THE Chinese are coming
    Being in China and
effect on my life. I will
their Bibles and the gentle tears that flowed as they prayed.
They live simple yet miraculous lives and through these pages
you too can meet the Chinese church. Read this book and let
their courage challenge you; the miracles amaze you; and their
dedication inspire you to carry Jesus into our nations and see
revival here too.

Rachel Hickson
Founder, Heartcry For Change

For all those, like ourselves, who have followed the growth of
Christianity in China from afar, this is an inspirational book.
Over the decades since China closed its doors as a nation, we
have had to content ourselves with occasional stories leaking
out of church growth and accompanying persecution.

    Now that China in the twenty-first century is rising as a
world power, it seems that Chinese Christianity is rising with it!
It has been estimated that more people go to church in China
than belong to the Communist party. If this is so, then surely
Christianity has played its part in the growing confidence,
economic growth, and international stature of this huge nation
of China.

    This book will show you some of the roots and shoots of
what God is doing in China today! May it inspire much prayer.

Roger and Faith Forster
Founders of the Ichthus Christian Fellowship

This book reminds us again why we are fascinated by the history
of the Chinese Church and the perseverance of its saints, for
it captures the essence of God's passion for all of us and His
profound plans for the future of our world. The mission of
these saints to take the gospel "Back to Jerusalem" will be strewn
with much suffering and pain. That is why our fervent prayers
and support in all forms must be given with equal measure of
passion and zeal to match their courage.

Tan Sri Dr Francis Yeoh
Managing Director, YTL Corporation

This is a really important book, based on some intensive in-country research of the history and testimonies from the last generation of courageous Chinese missionaries, and then looking at the remarkable fruit of their ministry, and the implications for the world missionary movements. The Chinese are coming! I highly recommend this for your inspiration and encouragement.

Gordon Hickson
Chairman of Love China International and National Coordinator of Mahabba Network International

History is "His story"! Jesus Christ came personally into the world to die for men's sins, and now He calls on His servants to spread the gospel throughout the whole earth so that His work of salvation can be completed. It was through His faithful servants that the gospel came to the ancient land of China, and the perseverance and endurance of His servants even to the point of death, that has allowed the Chinese Church to grow and be established. For this we in China are exceedingly grateful!

My hope is that through the testimonies and the message of this book, those brothers and sisters who have all served China in hundreds of different ways may see the fruits of their labour and find reassurance that none of their efforts in Christ have been in vain. These stories are just an offering of firstfruits to God. My longing is that by the grace of God the Chinese Church might join hands with the rest of the world to spread the gospel with even more power and effectiveness, bringing even more glory to God!

Pastor Wang
Chairman of Beijing House Church Leaders' Forum

THE COMING CHINESE CHURCH

How Rising Faith in China
Is Spilling Over Its Boundaries

Paul Golf

with

Pastor Lee

MONARCH
BOOKS

Oxford, UK & Grand Rapids, Michigan, USA

Published by Monarch Books
an imprint of
Lion Hudson plc
Wilkinson House, Jordan Hill Road,
Oxford OX2 8DR, England
Email: monarch@lionhudson.com
www.lionhudson.com/monarch

ISBN 978 0 85721 331 0
e-ISBN 978 0 85721 475 1

First edition 2013

Acknowledgments
All Scripture quotations taken from the Holy Bible, Today's New
International Version. Copyright © 2004 by International Bible
Society. Used by permission of Hodder & Stoughton Publishers.
A member of the Hachette Livre UK Group. All rights reserved.
"TNIV" is a registered trademark of International Bible Society.
Scripture quotations marked ESV are from The Holy Bible, English
Standard Version® (ESV®) copyright © 2001 by Crossway, a
publishing ministry of Good News Publishers. All rights reserved.
Scripture quotations marked HCSB are from the Holman Christian
Standard Bible copyright © 2004 Holman Bible Publishers. All rights
reserved.

A catalogue record for this book is available from the British Library

Printed and bound in the UK, October 2013, LH26

Contents

Author's Preface

Offering a faithful and representative view of the Chinese Church in the twenty-first century is no simple task. Many books have already been written on the spread of Christianity in China, and many differing and at times starkly contrasting interpretations have been offered.

My own position as an author is somewhat unusual in that I am not a missionary, China-watcher, sociologist, or even someone who has spent extensive periods of time with the Chinese House Churches. From very early on in my Christian life, something implanted itself deep in my spirit concerning this mysterious civilization on the other side of the world and what God might be doing there. Somehow I found myself with the conviction that whatever it was, it would be deeply significant and instrumental in shaping the world of the new millennium. Even so, no one was more surprised than me when I found God calling me to invest four years of my life in studying Mandarin Chinese at Oxford University instead of attending theological college as was my intention.

It was through connecting with Gordon Hickson in Oxford that I was first introduced to Pastor Lee, the director of Love China International, described to me by Gordon as a *world changer*. Since completing my master's degree in conference interpreting and translation, I have had the privilege to work with Pastor Lee and his wife as both a translator and as a minister, seeking to create a bridge between the Church of East and West. The message and content of this book is an eclectic mix distilled from countless interviews, ministry trips, and late-night conversations with a wide spectrum of individuals, some of which have involved me, but all of which have involved Pastor Lee.

This seeks to be a prophetic book, looking not only to examine China's history or even its present, but asking God to breathe His revelation on its future. Although I am honoured to lend my abilities as a writer in giving a voice to that message, the credit for its substance belongs to the thousands of Chinese Church leaders, Western missionaries, and to Pastor Lee himself, who have all in unique ways laid down their lives in response to the call of God, and who in return have been entrusted with *those secret things of God*, each with different coloured tiles in the grand mosaic of revelation. For the sake of clarity, where the book refers to "we" or "us", it is talking about Pastor Lee and myself and unless otherwise stated, "I" or "me" refers to the author.

It is almost impossible to present a generalized picture of what God is doing among 1.4 billion people, and many differing opinions abound both within China itself and among the International Church community. In general terms, however, I believe it is fair to say that one of the key values of Chinese Christianity is the commitment to unity, or as the apostle Paul calls it *the Oneness of the Spirit*. We ask that you read this book with an open heart and receive it with the spirit of humility in which we have sought to write it. It is impossible to give due time to all those whose lives and ministries have been used by God in His work in China, and so while the scope of this book may seem grand, it only seeks to be one piece of the puzzle. May Abba God bless you profoundly, explode your vision, and raise your faith in what He is able to do as you read it!

Paul Golf
March 2013

Pastor Lee's Preface

I often go to China to give our brothers and sisters in Christ there training or support, but every time it is in fact me who comes away changed, having been humbled by their simple faith and devotion to ministry. My last few visits have been to support the writing of this book, conducting interviews and research with our brothers and sisters in Christ.

Through the years I have been travelling there, I have come to believe that God has given the Chinese Church two main weapons, the first being praise and worship. In the churches there, instruments are seldom found, but hours of songs learned by heart can be heard in rousing a cappella voices. The Canaan Hymns series of over 1,000 songs was gathered by Xiao Min, a woman who is unable to read music, but has been blessed with a gift of songwriting. Her story may be extraordinary, but it is just one example of God's work in China and his continuing blessing on their praise and worship.

Secondly, the Chinese churches have a strong prayer life that I have experienced at first hand. Every building used as a church will have a prayer room, and 24-hour prayer circles are commonplace; this is a weapon that brings breakthrough and miracles. I believe these gifts have been given by the Lord who knows that the power of prayer and worship is needed to take the gospel into the hard lands of the Old Silk Road, and back to Jerusalem.

The Chinese Church can have this dedication partly because of the legacy left by the sacrifices of the early Western missionaries, some of whom gave their lives in the spreading of the gospel. The model that they left for the Chinese was one to aspire to, and we must not forget this. We want this book to link the Chinese and Western churches in the pursuit of the "Back to Jerusalem" vision. We believe the Western Church can be raised up and once more be linked with the Chinese Church to carry the gospel back to Jerusalem.

Finally, we would like to use this book to express thanks for the support we have received throughout the years, without which we wouldn't be able to do this ministry. Thank you to the prayer warriors, to those who have aided our work in China financially, and of course to my family – my wife, son, and daughter – who are always my first and firmest foundation.

Pastor Lee

Foreword by Brother Yun

The Heavenly Man would like to strongly recommend that you read *The Coming Chinese Church*! The Bible says, *God will save the descendants of Abraham.*

I am an elder from the Chinese House Church, known as "Brother Yun, the Heavenly Man". I have also been involved in promoting the Back to Jerusalem vision around the world. I have been arrested and detained many times, and imprisoned for more than fourteen years on account of the gospel of Jesus Christ. Today I would like to earnestly recommend this book, *The Coming Chinese Church*, to you before God.

In former times God sent forth missionaries into China to sow the seeds of the gospel of love. Now it is time for China to do the same.

We, the "Coming Chinese Church", not only want to thank and honour the Western missionaries who went out into China sowing in tears, paying the price for the gospel of Jesus Christ with their own blood, but also to give glory to God for the missionary vision handed down to us from Him through those Western missionaries many years ago – Go West with the gospel! *This gospel of the kingdom must be preached in all nations as a testimony to them.* This is the heart of the Back to Jerusalem vision! The Coming Chinese Church is now beginning to heed Christ's call to train and send out squadrons of missionaries into East Asia and the Middle East, to take the message of true love into these regions and extend the kingdom of God, but there are also a great many young Chinese Christians who have fixed their heart on the call of God, and are studying hard to perfect their foreign languages and come as missionaries to Europe, America, and Great Britain. These men and women called by God believe that these nations are our spiritual Abraham. We are all just mere men formed from the dust of the ground, and the Western nations have misused religion, politics, and the power of man so that those ancient living wells of faith have seemingly been blocked up by dirt and stones. Because of their faith in Jesus Christ, the Coming Chinese Church is like your spiritual Isaac, come to help re-dig those ancient wells so that the living stream of life would once again flow freely!

Thank you Jesus! Many churches in the UK, Europe, and America have been awakened by God to work together with the Coming Chinese Church and the Back to Jerusalem vision to see the kingdom of God advance. I firmly believe that the publication of this book will have a great impact on many churches, even thoroughly changing the concepts of what mission means to the Eastern and Western Church to bring about a new movement of revival and reformation. I cannot recommend highly enough that anyone who has a heart for the kingdom of God or for missions would take the time to read *The Coming Chinese Church*!

The Heavenly Man, Brother Yun
A Leader from the Chinese House Church

1

China's Kairos Moment

It was Easter 1942. Pastor Dai had divided us into groups and sent us to churches all over Shaanxi province. I had gone with Dr Mark and Brother Zheng Guang'en to Baoji city. Our plan was to hold some meetings for Easter. At Dr Mark's suggestion we rose before dawn and had gone down to the river to celebrate the Lord's resurrection. While we were praying, God showed us a vision concerning the future of the Church. In the vision was a huge lake. There were people from many nations coming to it: Americans, British, French, Swedish, Norwegians. The water of the gospel was pouring into the lake through a great many channels in a multitude of rushing streams. However, no matter how much water poured forth, the lake was never filled. Pastor Mark prayed, "Lord, what does the vision mean? With so many inlets of water this lake should be full to overflowing, but it isn't! How can this be?" The Lord spoke to us clearly, "This is your Church, the Church of China." When we heard this we were stunned. How could this be? The Lord spoke again, "You take in the light, but there is no reflection. My word to you now is this: the Chinese Church must go out with the gospel."

Mrs He Enzheng, born 1916, of the Back to
Jerusalem Evangelistic Band

On 6 May 2011, a man and his wife were checking in through security at Beijing International Airport. The border guard looked at the photograph in the woman's passport, running it through the electronic scanning machine linked to the government's national security database. After a few tense moments, he handed her back her passport. *You're clear to go through*, he said. Anxiously she waited on the other side of the security barrier, looking back at her husband. Another passport slid through the scanning machine, and again came those tense moments of waiting. Suddenly a frown came across the guard's face. *I'm sorry*, he said to the man. *Your name is on a list of people who are not allowed to leave the country. Your passport is invalid; you have to go home.*

In shock, Mrs Gao watched as the guard pulled out a giant pair of scissors and cut through the cover of her husband's passport. With only a short window of time to spare, Brother Gao spoke to his wife across the barrier. He encouraged her to go on without him, and with a tearful goodbye she turned and in a daze proceeded into the departure lounge to board her plane. It seemed as if she would now have to go alone on the scheduled five-week ministry tour of Europe. Her first destination: Paris, Charles de Gaulle International Airport.

For many years the House Churches of China have been almost legendary among the body of Christ in the Western world. Brother Yun's testimony as recorded in the book *The Heavenly Man* brought a fresh insight into the world of Chinese Christianity, highlighting especially the fierce persecution and incredible trials that thousands of believers have endured under the hostile Communist regime. Many others have been inspired by stories of tens of thousands of Chinese people being ushered into the kingdom on a daily basis, or have been touched by the testimonies of missionaries, well-known and lesser-known, of how God has been moving in astounding and miraculous ways across this *nation of many nations*. All too often, however, these stories of a God who is transforming individuals, communities, and nations, a God of manifest glory and demonstrable signs and wonders, are relegated to the status of modern Christian mythology so far removed from the experience of many Western believers as to be alien to them.

The China of the 1940s was a place of great turmoil. Following the overthrow of the last Qing emperor in 1911 and the establishment of the new government, thirty years of chaos had torn the country apart through warlordism, Japanese invasion, and civil conflict. Against this uncertain backdrop, Western missionaries had been sowing their lives for the cause of the gospel within China's fragile borders. A small but substantial contingent of Chinese believers had been built up in key areas around China. The vision they saw of the Church in China was not a vision of defeat, or of dependence upon foreign ministers to carry the torch of the gospel on their behalf, but of a great army of believers who would pour out from China in obedience to Jesus' commission to take His light *into all the earth*. They understood the biblical principle that *much is demanded from those to whom much has been given*, and seeing the sacrifice of so many foreign missionaries on their behalf, they came to recognize that God had placed a call and a responsibility on the Chinese Church to become like the church in Antioch, taking the gospel to the unreached world.

The China of today is almost completely unrecognizable when compared with the 1940s, but that same vision and passion to look beyond oneself to see the kingdom of God established on earth is still very much present, just as it was for missionaries such as Hudson Taylor and Gladys Aylward who gave their lives to China.

The technical term used by the Chinese government for believers such as Brother Gao and his wife who seek to obey the Great Commission is, like many Chinese terms, somewhat blunt and to the point: *Leaders of the Occult*. Brother Gao is the pastor of a network of churches in one of the bigger cities in China. He and his wife had been invited to preach in a series of churches and conference meetings across Europe in May 2011. This was an unprecedented move. A national leader in the Chinese House Church had never before been able to minister openly in Europe in such a high-profile manner and return safely to China afterwards. Under the regime of the Chinese Communist Party, any religious activity is subject to a series of strict controls. It has now become quite well known outside China that the only *legal* way to be a practising Christian or church member in China is to be part of the government operated, or so-called *Three-Self* Church. Generally speaking, Christians in China who, for whatever reason, do not want to be subject to the restrictions in the state Church make up what is often termed the Chinese House Church. As an unregistered House Church pastor, it is unsurprising that Brother Gao encountered some problems leaving the country. What happened next, however, was quite unprecedented.

Halfway around the world, we were preparing to conduct our European ministry tour without our main speaker from China. It is generally received wisdom that bringing leaders out from the Chinese Church to preach in an open conference setting is at best risky and at worst impossible, but we had sensed that God wanted to shift something in the dynamic between the Eastern and Western churches and that there was something very spiritually significant in trying. Over the following two weeks, Brother Gao went into a period of fasting and praying while our network of ministry partners and intercessors began to pray for God to work a miracle. Amazingly, within a few days the Chinese government reversed their decision to block his exit from China and issued him with a new passport. As his interpreter, I flew to Paris to meet Brother Gao and bring him to London where we would conduct our first series of meetings at the famous Emmanuel Centre on Marsham Street.

As I sat with Brother Gao on the inter-terminal train to connect with our flight to the UK, he asked me if I knew why God had not allowed him to come two weeks earlier when he had been separated from his wife at the airport. I didn't know the answer to that question, but then he proceeded to tell me how during the previous two weeks, God had begun to speak to him about a great revival coming to the United Kingdom, which would spread throughout the whole of Europe. As someone who is very interested in revival, that really got my attention! While he was waiting for his appeal to be considered, he had felt prompted by the Holy Spirit to start studying the lives of the nineteenth-century missionaries who went out from Europe – and especially the United Kingdom – to China. He shared how astounded he was by their love for China and their commitment to the gospel. *God says that His gifts and His calling are irrevocable*, he told me.

> *For that promise to be fulfilled, Europe has to rise up again into her apostolic destiny. I myself am a spiritual descendant of those missionaries who gave their lives for China, and the Chinese Church has been grown from the seeds left behind by their service and their faith. If I had come two*

weeks earlier I would not have been prepared for this trip, but God has used this time to show me the message I need to preach. The thing that the Chinese Church most needs right now is spiritual fathers, and we are looking to the Western churches with many generations of history to come alongside us.

Elijah and the Widow

In 1 Kings 17–19, we read the story of the prophet Elijah having a showdown with the false prophets of Baal and Asherah on Mount Carmel over who was the true God. In 2004 I was spending time at Beijing University studying Chinese on an overseas programme that was part of my degree. Within a few weeks of being in the city, God had introduced me to Christians from a House Church in Beijing. One particular believer, called Peter, and I became good friends, and we began to meet regularly to pray. On one afternoon we were sitting in a park and I suggested to him that we go somewhere more private to seek God together. He paused for a moment and then told me he thought he knew a place where we could go. He took out his mobile phone and made a call to someone, although with my limited knowledge of Chinese at that time I didn't understand what they were saying. As we took a short taxi ride to another part of the city, he said to me that if anyone asks I should say that we have been friends for a long time. At that point I realized that the call he had made was to a

House Church pastor to see if they would be willing to risk having a white foreigner come to one of their meetings. When I suggested that we find a place to pray, I thought we might go to a quiet cafe somewhere, not to a meeting of Underground Church believers!

We arrived at a dilapidated old apartment block in a section of the city not commonly known for foreign faces. As we went up to a fourth-floor apartment, Peter knocked on the door and was greeted by a pair of eyes peering around a chain lock. When they recognized him, the door closed again, unlocked, and they beckoned us in. I saw a group of perhaps fifty believers all crammed into a living room listening to a visiting preacher. When I walked in, I have to confess that I was absolutely terrified! I had heard that it was virtually impossible for Western Christians to be given access to underground meetings, and I reckoned that the believers who were in there must have thought I was some kind of important missionary to be allowed to come in. If it were not hard enough to keep a low profile as the only six-foot-tall white man in a room crammed full of Chinese, the only space for me to sit was right at the front next to the preacher, and everyone had to wait as I picked my way through the chairs to get to my seat. The preacher turned to me and asked me in an American accent if I understood Mandarin. Although my Chinese was fairly elementary I just nodded and said *Yes. Good, then I don't have to translate*, he replied. For the next half an hour I sat there with my heart in my mouth, unable to understand virtually anything the preacher was saying and half convinced that at any moment the Public Security Bureau might burst through the door. At one point a lady began to cry, apparently touched in some profound way by the message. I was struck by the love and compassion in his voice as he prayed for her, although I still didn't understand most of what was said.

At the end of the meeting, I was introduced to a mix of people. Migrant workers from poor backgrounds mixed with master's students from the nearby university. Several were not yet Christians, invited by their friends to come and hear the gospel. Some commotion took place at the back, and the preacher was hastily whisked away from the apartment. The hospitality of the church was amazing, as the lady pastor invited me to join them as an honoured guest for dinner at a local restaurant after they had dispersed. My friend Peter told me how he had become a Christian after God raised him from the dead, and how, as a young man growing up without a father, God had been the father to him that he so desperately needed. I asked him if they were not afraid of the government, and I'll never forget his answer as he looked at me with a wry smile and a slight squint: *If you fear God, you don't have to fear the government!*

A few days later, we sat together in a basement cafeteria in one of the big market malls common throughout cities in China. He asked me to share a message from God for him. Put on the spot, I asked the Holy Spirit what I should say, and instantly I sensed Him lead me to the story of Elijah. Taking out my English Bible and Chinese Bible, I began to preach to my friend about the story of Elijah calling down fire from heaven on Mount Carmel. All of a sudden, Peter became very excited and jumped up out of his seat. *That's exactly what China needs!* he exclaimed in a tone loud enough to draw the attention of surrounding customers (not to mention the security guard with the automatic weapon a few tables away).

> *China needs Elijahs! I used to be just like Elijah, but I'm not as on fire as I used to be. Once when I was reading the Bible, the light bulb above my head blew out and I was so angry with the bulb for obscuring the word of God that I looked up, and commanded the bulb to come back on in the name of Jesus — and it did! China desperately needs Elijahs! Next week, you and I have to go back to the church and preach this message to them!*

Then he started preaching the gospel to the noodle lady serving food at one of the counters, again just loud enough to remind me of that security guard standing nearby!

Nine years later, and I have only recently understood the significance of that conversation. I believe that my friend spoke prophetically by the Holy Spirit when he exclaimed that China needs Elijahs. When I discussed with Pastor Lee how it would be best to begin this book, he shared with me the revelation that God had given him concerning the relationship between the Chinese and Western churches. In 1 Kings 17, God speaks to Elijah after the drought has begun and calls him to go and visit the widow of Zarephath.

Elijah is tired from his journey and worn out, but God has sustained him in the midst of massive spiritual decline in the nation. God didn't ask him to go to someone who had the means to support Elijah, but to someone who was desperately in need herself. She was poor, without anyone to help her, and with only one meal left. To human logic, it would seem totally counterintuitive to send Elijah to such a person. When he reaches Zarephath, he finds the widow gathering sticks to prepare a fire and cook the final meal for her and her son. He asks her first to make the sacrifice of giving him a small loaf of bread in faith that God would then provide supernaturally for her and her family. The widow agrees, and God is faithful in blessing them with an ever-replenishing supply of oil and flour for the duration of the drought.

The Chinese Church is still the fastest growing in the world, but spiritually speaking and in terms of the administration of the Church and the nation, they are desperately in need. They are faced with an uncertain future and a rapidly changing environment. Through many conversations with Chinese Christians, church pastors, young people, or families, it is clear that the excitement of revival in their country is mixed with a deep sense of feeling lost, without an identity or guarantee of provision. They are like the poor widow that God called Elijah to go and see. Meanwhile the Western Church is like Elijah, seeking to maintain their Christian witness in a secularized society. Many people in the West have a hunger to hear about what God is doing in China. Is it simple curiosity, or an empathy with the stories of persecuted believers? Perhaps it is a growing desire for God to move in the same incredible ways once again in their own nations? Chances are if you are reading this book it is because something in you is drawn in faith towards what God is doing in China.

I think that to begin with, neither Elijah nor the widow knew why God had called them together. The widow was looking for outside help, but God would have her first look to Elijah's need. God is saying to the Chinese Church that, like the widow, they must look beyond themselves to meet the needs of others. While they are still looking for support, they themselves have something to give. A time is coming on the horizon when the drought of persecution and hardship will fully pass away in China, and God has planned for the Elijah of the Western Church to once again face down the false prophets in the land with a dramatic demonstration of the Spirit's power. In the account of the story, the widow's son dies and she gives him to Elijah for God to work a miracle. The future destiny of the Chinese Church requires the right relationships with the spiritual fathers of the Western Church in order to survive into maturity. We believe that in this hour, God is creating a bridge between the churches of East and West, to supply one another and encourage one another in what God is doing so as to prepare for what He is about to do next in the earth. May this book be a refreshment to the Western Church, and an encouragement to the Chinese to look beyond their own borders to the hills of their future.

Understanding the Times

Kairos is a Greek word that refers to a particular instance or strategic moment in time. When we are used to an overly individualistic spirituality, we can overlook the fact that God's move in the earth is all part of His grand design. In C. S. Lewis's allegory *The Great Divorce*, the people of the shadowy world argued with one another over the times and seasons in which they were living. Because the passing of one day in their world took many thousands of years, the people couldn't agree if the perpetual twilight they experienced was a sign that the sun was rising or setting. The two futures couldn't be further apart. One would be an era of daylight, while the other would be plunged into darkness. Their problem was that they could only see the moment, divorced from the continuity of history and blind to the revelation of the future. If only they were able to understand the narrative of their own story and the context of their moment in time, they would have been able to prepare successfully for the next season.

I am often asked by people what the secret of the Chinese Church is. What do they have that has allowed for such amazing growth over the past few decades? In case the China Miracle has passed you by, here are a few facts and figures:

When the Chinese Communist Party declared the establishment of New China in 1949, Christianity was effectively declared a criminal, counter-revolutionary ideology. One of the foundational tenets of Marxist philosophy says that religion is a system of control that would die away and become redundant if only the repressed underclasses could gain social emancipation and material prosperity. Chairman Mao and the Communist Party believed that religion of all forms should be eradicated and outside influences that might pollute the Communist ideology of a new nation should be fiercely guarded against. For the next three decades, the whole country was all but closed to outside investigators. During this time, many observers in the Western world assumed that Christianity had been all but extinguished by the totalitarian oppression of the new regime. When China began to open up in the 1980s, the truth that there was a prolific, vital Church continuing to grow and operate despite fierce persecution came as a total surprise to much of the international Christian community, not to mention the secular world.

What is even more staggering is the scale of the growth during this period. The best estimates place the number of Chinese Christians in 1949 to be somewhere around the 800,000 mark. Just under sixty-five years later, the most cautiously conservative estimates would put the number at no fewer than 80,000,000. In fact this number is so conservatively low as to be ridiculous, but we will look into this in more detail in the next chapter. The point we are trying to make is that the Chinese Church, in a sixty-year period, under varying degrees of oppression and persecution by an institutionally atheist state, grew in size a hundredfold.

Hopefully this book will go some way as to shed light on some of the factors that have contributed to this incredible revival, but with just a summary glance at the strengths found among Chinese believers, three things stand out to me: They know how to believe, they know how to pray, and they know where they came from. Different apostolic and prophetic leaders in China have slightly different models through which they understand China's spiritual history, but there is a common understanding that God has been working with a specific strategy in mind through different seasons of the past few generations. We are going to look at five specific stages based on Israel's rebuilding of the desolate towns in 2 Chronicles 14:7. These are the building of walls, towers, gates, bars for the gates, and finally the taking of the land:

> *"Let us build up these towns," he said to Judah, "and put **walls** around them, with **towers**, **gates** and **bars**. The **land** is still ours, because we have sought the LORD our God; we sought him and he has given us rest on every side." So they built and prospered.*

2

The Hundred Million Revival

When we look at the history of the modern Chinese Church, we can see three distinct seasons. The first was a period of intense suffering and persecution, from 1949 until 1979. The second was from 1979 to 2000, when China was opening up and undergoing reform. This third season is the era of world mission for the Chinese Church.

Pastor Shen Xianfeng, Founder,
Zhongfu Network

The Fastest Growing Church in the World

Several years ago, a friend of mine was involved in some missionary work in a school in China. While he was staying there, a couple from Germany who were also helping out on the project called their family back home in Germany. As they were speaking on the phone, an irritated voice cut in on their conversation, saying, *Speak English, we can't understand you!*

Similarly, in the last few years I met with a Chinese pastor in the USA who had recently made an apparently low-profile trip into China to connect with some local church leaders there. After several hours sitting together in a street cafe, he was very surprised to discover that his phone was ringing – when it was a number that he hadn't even given out to anyone for security reasons. On the other end of the line was the Public Security Bureau (PSB) agent who had been assigned to follow him. The agent was waiting in a car over the road and had been listening in on their whole conversation with some hi-tech surveillance equipment. They had spent far too long talking and he was now bored, tired, and wanted to go home, so he hacked into the pastor's phone and asked him if they wouldn't mind hurrying things up so he could finish work for the day!

It is one of the worst kept secrets in Beijing that an unassuming high-rise office block in the downtown district serves as the main centre for several thousand employees of the PSB's listening post. Their job is to lend an ear to the phone calls, Skype conversations, emails, or SMS messages belonging to people who appear on the government's watch list, or which have been otherwise flagged up for illegal or politically sensitive content. China has one of the largest intelligence services in the world. There is a famous political slogan in China that the country runs on a system of *socialism, with Chinese characteristics*, which in effect means not really very socialist at all anymore, but we don't want to lose face by admitting it. This is what we might call *espionage, with Chinese characteristics*, in the sense that when most other countries try to hide the fact that they might spy on their citizens from time to time, the Chinese PSB assumes that you know you're being spied on and so doesn't go to great lengths to try to hide the fact. The habit among many church leaders is that when you hear that strange echo begins to cut in on your phone conversation, it's a great opportunity to share the gospel with the young university graduate who is more than likely bored to tears while listening away to your conversation in that third-floor office surrounded by the haze of Beijing smog!

Where there is a great deal more freedom and openness in Chinese society now than almost ever before, the past has all too often been filled with hardship and persecution for the fledgling Chinese Church, and many Chinese church leaders believe that a fresh wave of persecution is again on the horizon. Beginning in 1949, the Church experienced its worst era of opposition from the state. Bibles were banned, and Christians were routinely sent to labour camps for *counter-revolutionary thought.* Some were martyred for their faith, and others had to endure the shame of coming from families where one or more members had been branded an enemy of national harmony, or a *running dog of capitalism.* The fledgling Chinese Church was left to fend for itself in the midst of a long, hard winter. Even so, through it all many believers held on to their faith in Christ while continuing to practise their religion as best they could, and the Church continued to survive while many of the key leaders suffered in prison camps for refusing to renounce their faith.

... Put walls around them...

China became to all intents and purposes a closed country. In 1950, all foreign missionaries were expelled and 150 years of the missionary work that was pioneered by Robert Morrison, the first Protestant missionary to China, came to an end. In 1953, the Three-Self Patriotic Movement (TSPM) was formed by the Chinese government. Three-Self is short hand for Self-Governing, Self-Supporting, and Self-Propagating. The goal of this organization at its inception was to try to isolate the Chinese Christian believers from outside influences. The Marxist agenda under which the new government was operating expected religion as a whole and Christianity specifically to steadily vanish once the ties with Western imperial powers had been severed. The TSPM allowed Christians freedom to worship as long as they submitted the governance of the Church to the Communist Party, and agreed to be subject to many restrictions including a ban on evangelism, strict monitoring and censorship of the teaching content, and holding religious gatherings only in government designated locations at approved times.

It is impossible to gauge exactly how many Christians there are in China today. We mentioned briefly in the previous chapter that an extremely conservative estimate would put the number at no fewer than 80,000,000. In fact, the official statistics show a figure that is far higher. The government acknowledges a membership of around 21,000,000 in the Three-Self official Church. Catholicism is designated as a separate religion with a membership of 5,000,000 in the Three-Self Catholic Church. In 2011, the Chinese government publicly, albeit unofficially, admitted that the number of Christian believers in the (technically illegal) Protestant House Churches had exceeded the number of members of the Chinese Communist Party. The Party membership now stands at a little over 80,000,000, which means that even if you accept there to be some crossover between Three-Self and House Church membership a figure of 100,000,000 committed Christians is a reasonable estimate. In fact, in January 2007, the Chinese State Administration for Religious Affairs acknowledged a figure as high as 130,000,000 including both Protestants and Catholics.

When in 1979 Deng Xiaoping's economic reforms brought about a new level of freedom in Chinese society, the gospel exploded throughout the countryside as if a volcanic pressure were suddenly allowed to vent. The Church caught fire, with many ordinary, uneducated people blazing a trail of missionary fervour throughout China's countryside. One testimony recalls a young woman who had vowed to preach the gospel to at least one person every day of her Christian life. One winter she found herself in a village in Northern China, where the bitterly cold weather and early sunset meant that you could scarcely find anyone outside their own home. This woman had spent an entire day trying to find someone to share the gospel with, but evening had come and she had been unable to find a single person. Quite discouraged that this might be the first day since she became a Christian that she hadn't been able to share her faith, she began to get ready for bed. As she braved the cold and rain to use the wooden outhouse shared by the village, she suddenly heard a cough from the adjacent cubicle in the men's toilets. Excited, she knocked on the wall to see if anyone was there. A cautious and rather bemused reply came from the man on the other side. Not one to miss an opportunity, she asked him if anyone had ever told him about Jesus. He replied he had never heard of Jesus but he'd be happy to listen to her if she wanted to tell him, and so this young evangelist proceeded to do just that, finishing the evening by praying with the man to receive Christ as his saviour through the wooden wall of a village outhouse!

Although a high wall had been built around the nation, with precious little that could get in or out, many of the older generation of converts from the days of Protestant missions kept a hold on their faith in the midst of the worst years of oppression. In the end, it would seem that their prayers began to fill the void of spiritual anorexia fostered under Chairman Mao's famous axiom: *religion is a poison*.

The First Wave of Awakening

Something was stirring in the late 1970s and early 1980s. A new generation of House Church leaders was emerging on the scene without any affiliation to historical Protestant denominations. Several large networks began to form which would each grow to have a national membership numbering in the millions. They are sometimes referred to as the *Big Families* in Chinese. One of the oldest and most famous is the Fangcheng Fellowship, with a reported membership of over ten million as of 2010. On a similar scale is the Chinese Gospel Fellowship, sometimes called the Tanghe Fellowship, which was started by Pastor Shen Xianfeng. Over a period of thirty years, the fellowship has spread from Pastor Shen's native Henan province and has planted churches in every major city in the country.

Pastor Lee was able to spend some time with Pastor Shen, who was willing to share with us his extraordinary testimony as well as his insights into China's current situation and the future of the Church. He describes himself as a simple, rural Chinese preacher. From his youth he had been exposed to Christianity through his maternal grandparents, who had come to Christ through the ministry of the China Inland Mission, an organization founded by the British missionary Hudson Taylor. Not long after his grandparents became Christians, China's doors closed and all the Western ministers were expelled. There was no one left with a knowledge of the Bible or anything but the most rudimentary of Christian teaching. Shortly after that, even the churches built by the foreign missionaries were all burned to the ground, and those believers who remained were forced into meeting in secret in their homes. Only the remotest rural areas of provinces such as Wenzhou, Guizhou, and Yunnan still have church buildings that survive from this time. Most were either systematically destroyed or requisitioned by the government. The only knowledge of Scripture that they had access to was through the hymns and choruses that they could remember from the Western missionaries.

At the end of the 1970s, Shen was in his mid teens and preparing to graduate from upper-middle school when he fell seriously ill. Struck with a mystery illness, he found himself almost completely paralysed and unable to speak for days. Anxious classmates as well as his teachers would come to visit him, hoping to wish him well and help in any way that they could, but there seemed to be nothing that anyone was able to do. His entire life came to a standstill and the future looked very bleak. At the same time, his mother was diagnosed as being in the final stages of terminal cancer. Unable to eat and suffering terribly from diarrhoea and internal bleeding, she had one final wish: to go and see her parents to say her last goodbyes. Sensing that he also might not survive much longer, the young man agreed to accompany his mother back home. He described how they struggled to make the journey on foot, barely able to walk and weakened from the lack of food.

When they finally arrived, the grandparents were filled with compassion and began to share the gospel with them. Shen noted how tangible the sense of love that he felt from them was. This old couple said that the reason they had fallen ill was because their faith had been weakened by the teaching of Darwinism and atheism, and that their confidence in God had been shaken by the public denouncing and beating of Christians during the Cultural Revolution. His mother was deeply moved by their testimony and started to repent of her sins and give her life to Christ. As his grandparents prayed for her, she immediately felt in her body that she was healed and found she was able to eat again after many days without food. Shen was terrified as he watched her eat, as it might cause her to die at any moment, but since that day more than thirty years ago right up until her present age of seventy-nine, she has remained in exceptionally good health without ever having had any cancer treatment.

Amazed by what he saw, Shen also decided to surrender his life to Christ and in turn was completely healed. Countless miracles then began to take place all around the region, as if the floodgates had been opened. He recounted to us how he witnessed thousands of people being healed of all kinds of diseases, including cancer, blindness, and paralysis, and even those who were dead being brought back to life:

> We had such an encounter with the power of God
> [he said]. But our knowledge of the truth was so
> limited. I remember hearing the people shouting
> "hallelujah" and I asked them what it meant. I

*was a young man full of questions. They told me
that it was a word that you shouted to kill evil
spirits when you prayed for people to be healed!*

In fact, on many occasions they would just shout *hallelujah*
over people and they would be healed instantly. People
would talk about Jerusalem from half-remembered Bible
stories, but nobody knew where Jerusalem was. It sounded
to them like a phrase that Chinese farmers would chant
as they ploughed the field; something akin to *heave-ho the
plough*. Many didn't even realize that it was a real place!
Shen's desire for truth and frequent questioning were
mistaken for doubt, and he was told he should simply
believe in the power of God and stop asking questions.

It was through the ministry of Global Radio, a Christian
radio station broadcast into China, that he first heard
Christian teaching. *Although I had encountered the power of
God, I really came to know the Lord through the gospel radio
station. Not only was my physical body completely healed, but
my soul was healed too. I was so full of God's peace.* By 1980,
many of the older generation of believers who had survived
the Cultural Revolution began to come and hear him preach.
There was such a hunger in them for the word of God,
starved as they had been for nearly thirty years without any
access to Scriptures or Christian literature. Because he had
attended school, Shen was able to make written notes on
all the messages that he heard from the radio broadcasts. To
begin with, when people came to him, he simply repeated
the messages to them from the notes he had taken. For his

hearers, it was as if the ember of a long-neglected flame began to glow again. They brought their children and grandchildren to hear the preaching of the gospel, and countless families gave their lives to Christ across three generations.

Then in 1983, a massive wave of persecution came. The Public Security forces had become aware that mass conversions to Christianity were taking place throughout many rural areas. The entire Christian community suffered during this time, but the primary target was invariably those like Pastor Shen who could be identified as leaders. Most people had no access to Scripture at all, and many of the few who did were unable to understand it, as literacy levels were still very low. Their task was not an easy one because, with a total of over 50,000 written characters including 3,000 in common usage, Chinese is undoubtedly the most complicated written language in the world! As persecution grew more severe, Shen found himself forced to leave the area. Since then he has never returned to his home village.

He and the group who escaped with him were mostly young people. They had no idea where they were supposed to go, but such a Holy Spirit passion gripped them that they went wherever they were able and preached the gospel from town to town. Countless miracles followed them, and word spread that the sick were being healed. Upon entering a new area they would first try to find out if any old believers were still alive there. Many of them had continued to pray faithfully for China throughout the years of hardship and were glad to offer their homes to the travelling preachers for as long as possible. The gospel began to spread first within families, as wives shared the gospel with their husbands, children with parents, and from one cousin to another. Neighbours and friends would encourage each other to come and listen to him preach. In a three-year period, they planted no fewer than 500 churches, but to Shen the reason is clear: *It was all the work of the Holy Spirit. We are all sons and daughters of God, and He is able to move through us all.*

This period abounds with similar stories of young preachers and evangelists moving from one town to the next, preaching until persecution drove them onwards. The authorities thought that if they opposed the leaders and denied people access to Scripture their faith would collapse. While many suffered terribly under these attacks, it only meant that the Chinese Church was forced to develop a very simple, passionate, and pure faith. Their theology consisted of giving your life to Jesus, being baptized, healing the sick, and telling others about it. Many future church leaders would come to Christ during this revival. Brother Yun's testimony is also focused mainly around this period. Pastor Lee has a friend in China who still remembers as a young child when Brother Yun came to preach in his village. Witnessing the dozens of miracles of healing and dramatic conversions has had a profound effect on him. Now in his thirties, he is still passionately following Christ himself, and is leading a church and a missionary training centre in Wenzhou. The furnace of persecution refined the faith of the Chinese believers, free from the disunity, denominationalism, and institutionalization that have beset so many other churches throughout history. It was a black and white world, with a clear enemy in the ruling authorities, and a clear mission in seeing China saved.

The Churches Multiply

While there are leaders who grew to stand out in this season, it was an entire generation of mostly young people who were the catalyst for such tremendous revival in China's countryside in the 1980s. Pastor Shen recalls one occasion when they had planted between ten and twenty churches in and around one particular village. Every evening they would hold evangelistic meetings and pray for the sick. A little while later, he travelled back to the same region and discovered that dozens more churches had sprung up throughout all the neighbouring townships, and people were coming from all over the area to hear him preach. He asked the local elders who had gone to preach in all of these places. *You did*, they replied. Shen was quite puzzled by their response as he was certain that he had never set foot in any of the areas where these hundreds of new believers were coming from. When he enquired further, he discovered that someone had brought a tape recorder into his meetings during his first trip, and now copies of his sermons had been distributed throughout the whole region. *I never told those people to go out and evangelize in that way*, he said. *It was the Holy Spirit who inspired them to do it, not me.*

The healings and miracles remained a vital part of the ministry. In one village there was a child who was suffering from liver failure. To look at him you could tell that he was close to death. The family brought him to the gospel meeting and laid him down while the people sang and listened to the message. By the time the meeting had finished, the boy had been completely healed. In many cases such as this, the sick and dying were cured just as they listened to the gospel being preached without anyone praying for them.

By the mid 1980s, they were planting churches on a daily basis. No one is able to say how many churches were established all across China in a similar fashion at this time, or how many people came to Christ every day. They would baptize a minimum of 1,000 people at once, often in freezing cold rivers during the winter months so as to minimize the chance of detection by the authorities. *Many people were healed even as they were baptized. All of these things were the fruits of God's blessing among us.*

The wall of persecution meant that the Church was forced out of complacency and into action. *Jesus said that when you are persecuted in one city, move on to the next,* explains Pastor Shen.

One day the PSB managed to find me in a region where we had seen high levels of growth within the Chinese Gospel Fellowship. They brought me in for a meeting, and asked if I would explain to them how come the Church was growing so fast in their area. My reply was in fact fairly tongue-

in-cheek – Really we owe it all to you guys! Look at it like this: Over these last ten years, your persecution of the Church has completely failed to destroy it. On the contrary, when you began to oppose us we moved from the countryside to the villages. If you come against us in the villages, we end up in the towns. When you persecuted us in the towns, we spread throughout the whole province. If you keep on going there, then sooner or later we will even get into the provincial capital city. If you still persecute us there, then there is nowhere left to go except home to heaven! Our job will be finished!

Pastor Shen's testimony, and many others like it, resembles that of the church in Jerusalem in Acts 8:1, *On that day a great persecution broke out against the church in Jerusalem, and all except the apostles were scattered throughout Judea and Samaria.* Jesus had given a mandate to the Church to go into all the world and preach the good news, but until the persecution came in Acts 8 they had not been obedient to this call, choosing instead to remain just in Jerusalem. The scattering caused by the outbreak of persecution forced all the believers to become missionaries! The wall of persecution may have been an obstacle in some ways, but in other ways it was a form of protection, allowing the Church to grow indigenously without outside influence, maintaining a purity of faith and conviction that is so easily lost in the modern world.

Power Encounters

A number of years ago I spent several months on an evening class called "Perspectives in the Worldwide Christian Movement", or "Perspectives" for short. If you haven't ever come across it then I cannot recommend it highly enough. One of the concepts I was introduced to on that course was that, in our applied theology of missions, we can see that in order for a person to truly become a disciple of Jesus they first need two kinds of encounters: truth encounters and power encounters. Truth is the reality of Christ explained, and power is the reality of Christ demonstrated. The evangelical view of missions has tended to major on leading people into truth encounters; that is to say the main focus is on preaching a gospel message that is accurate and doctrinally sound, with support from the ministry of apologetics which seeks to bring the light of reason to bear in defending the gospel. One of the problems that the Western evangelical Church has had to come to terms with is that postmodern culture is no longer that interested in talking about absolute truth. People want to know if something works first rather than if it is objectively "true".

Over the last twenty years, major revivals of a staggering nature have been seen all across the world. Few would have imagined at the beginning of China's Open Door Policy in 1979 that by the year 2000 Christianity would be growing faster in China than in any other nation in the world. Even fewer would have predicted that the second fastest would be the Islamic Republic of Iran, in which more than 10 per cent of the population now professes faith in Christ. These are extraordinary times! When we examine the new churches of the developing world that have grown exceptionally quickly in recent years, it is apparent that generally speaking the growth of theological and doctrinal knowledge has not been able to keep up with the rate at which the Church has been expanding numerically. This has been because wherever you see such high levels of growth, the accelerant seems to be healings and miracles or – especially in the case of the Islamic world – direct revelation of Jesus Christ through dreams and visions.

Nevertheless, without sound teaching revival is impossible to sustain. South Korea is one of the few nations in the last sixty years that has seen amazing revival grow to full maturity. They are now second only to the United States in terms of the number of missionaries that have been sent out worldwide. South Korea has been a major influence on the new generation of Chinese Church leaders, and they believe that, as the Chinese Church grows into maturity, they too will become one of the largest if not the largest missionary nation in history. One of the biggest obstacles to that dream, especially in those first twenty years of revival, has been the prevalence of false teachers and cults. Many believers of the Western Church lost their lives contending for the integrity of the gospel over many generations. The legacy and depth of spiritual insight and revelation that is the inheritance of the West is still desperately needed to help father and disciple the nations of the world that are only very young in the faith. Those nations in turn can teach us something about the simplicity of the gospel and the power of God. In 1 Corinthians 2:4, the apostle Paul said, *My message and my preaching were not with wise and persuasive words, but with a demonstration of the Spirit's power.* Have we in the Western Church become so preoccupied with being wise and persuasive that we have missed the power of the Spirit?

We don't understand the book of Acts, says Pastor Shen. *No one came and taught me the book of Acts, but I've lived it and I've experienced it. I think we are quite different to foreign churches. You seem to need to understand something before you go out and do it. For us, understanding only comes once we step out in faith. Every step that we took showed us what the Great Commission is all about. We never understood it in those terms, but we carried it out: Miracles, healings, being filled with the Holy Spirit, planting churches, ordaining elders, forming evangelistic teams – this is how the gospel spread over those twenty years!*

3

Foundations of Mission

You plan a tower that will pierce the clouds?
Lay first the foundation of humility…
The higher your structure is to be,
the deeper must be its foundation.

St Augustine

Thirteen-Hundred Years of History

Behind the walls of a closed nation, the Holy Spirit was tirelessly at work constructing great towers of faith that would soon rise above the walls to become visible from across the globe. The foundations of China's spiritual inheritance go back much further than the twentieth century, however. Among many evangelical Christians there is a sense that not much happened of note in China until the first Protestant missionaries arrived at the beginning of the nineteenth century. However, over 200 years before that, the Jesuit priest Matteo Ricci saw Catholicism make significant inroads into Chinese society. Ricci was famous for teaching new missionaries that they were there to introduce people to faith in Jesus Christ and not to try to convert their Chinese culture into a European one. The Chinese social and ethical system of Confucianism was, to him, mostly compatible with Christian teaching and shouldn't be preached against unless there was something in particular that was morally wrong or directly in conflict with the gospel. They even adopted Confucian terminology for God, rather than employing Western terminology, to make things more accessible to the Chinese.

Under Matteo Ricci's leadership, the Jesuits were very well received by the Kangxi Emperor, who welcomed missionaries who were versed in the sciences to join his royal court as special advisors. In 1692 he even issued an edict protecting Christian churches throughout the whole country, effectively elevating Christianity to the same level in Chinese society as the indigenous religions of Confucianism and Daoism. Ricci was not so popular with the Pope, however, who felt that the Jesuits were going too far in allowing Chinese converts to continue the practice of venerating their ancestors. Pope Clement XI issued a papal bull in 1715 forbidding Chinese Catholic converts to take part in Confucian rites, which outraged Kangxi to such a degree that the exasperated emperor expelled all of the Western missionaries from the country.

During Matteo Ricci's time in China, an artefact was uncovered which became known as the Nestorian

Stele. This is a ten-foot-high stone that dates back to the year AD 781. It records how 1,000 years before the Jesuit mission to China, a monk by the name of Alopen from the Church of the East was welcomed to China by the Tang Dynasty Emperor Taizong in AD 635. The first 150 years of Christian missions are summarized in the engraving on the stele, including teachings about the fall, the Trinity, and the coming of the Messiah. It then goes into detail concerning the ordination of bishops and erection of church buildings across the whole of China through several successive generations of emperors. The picture is one of a vibrant and active Christian community that made substantial inroads into Chinese society. Alopen is held to be responsible for the authorship and dissemination of the oldest of a group of writings called *The Jesus Sutras*, which convey Christian teaching, philosophy, and liturgy in a distinctly Chinese style, often utilizing terminology borrowed from Buddhism and Daoism to discuss elements of the gospel. When the stele was first discovered in the seventeenth century, the Chinese were amazed to discover that the religion being preached by the Jesuits was not a new introduction to China, but had first arrived more than a millennium before. By that time the Nestorian churches in China had gradually fallen into decline, along with the Church of the East as a whole, having been cut off and isolated from the Western Church through the upsurge of Islam in Asia.

Not until 150 years after the expulsion of the Jesuits did another missionary adopt a similarly radical approach to Chinese culture as Matteo Ricci. Hudson Taylor is famous for being the first Protestant missionary who was able to see the gospel advance into the inland areas of China. For the first fifty years of Protestant missions, work had focused almost exclusively on the coastal areas, where Chinese and foreigners would readily mix together through trade. Further inland, no one had ever seen a foreigner before, and Hudson Taylor realized that in order to reach these people he would need to work harder to bridge the gap between East and West. He started dressing in traditional Chinese robes and encouraged all of his missionaries to do the same. He was strikingly non-denominational in his approach, and would release people as missionaries, including single women, who had no formal theological qualifications. They were happy to conduct church meetings from house to house and did whatever possible to *become all things to all men* in order to reach the Chinese with the gospel. Despite his success, he earned no small amount of criticism from other missionary groups on account of his "unorthodox" approach.

Identity through Fatherhood

There is a word that consistently recurs in conversation with Chinese Church leaders: *chuancheng*. It literally means *to pass on and receive*. There is no direct equivalent in English, but the concept refers to the handing down of an inheritance through the generations. Psalm 145:4 says *One generation will declare your works to another* (HCSB).

It reflects the conviction that God's work in a particular generation of time does not stand alone, but is part of a much bigger plan that He has been putting into effect throughout many centuries. We cannot fully understand our identity or positioning in the grand scheme of things without recognizing and taking steps to appropriate our spiritual inheritance. The thing China needs more than anything else is the inheritance handed down by spiritual fathers. Many believers in China, especially of the older generation of church leaders, such as Shen Xianfeng, strongly identify themselves as the spiritual descendants of missionaries such as Hudson Taylor. The concept of *chuancheng* is key to making sense of what God is doing in China.

Ezra Jin is the senior pastor of Zion Church in Beijing and one of the foremost among a new generation of leaders in China. Originally he was converted in a Three-Self Church and went on to serve as an ordained TSPM minister. Eventually he left to establish Zion Church outside the official system. According to Ezra, when the Three-Self Church was established after 1949, those who wished to join had to first publicly denounce all Western missionaries as agents of foreign imperialism. In doing so, they dishonoured the spiritual heritage that was supposed to be theirs to take hold of. *The House Church mustn't allow its spiritual head to be cut off through politics*, he commented.

We need to give recognition to the Western missionaries who came to China and acknowledge

> *that the reason they came was because of the gospel,*
> *not out of an agenda to spread imperialism. They*
> *are our spiritual fathers. The inheritance passed*
> *down to us from them [chuancheng] was from*
> *God and not from man. For us in the Church*
> *today to answer the question "who are we?" then*
> *it is crucial for us to understand this. I met an old*
> *preacher from Guizhou who was brought to tears*
> *at the mention of the Western missionaries. "They*
> *gave their lives for China," he said. "How could*
> *we ever denounce them?" He went on to recite the*
> *story of how the missionary James Fraser gave all*
> *his medicine to the local people and lost his life to*
> *disease as a result.*

The British missionary James Fraser is a particular hero of the Chinese. He worked with the China Inland Mission among the Lisu tribe in south-west China and Burma from the early twentieth century until his death in 1938. Before his arrival, the tribe had no written language, which Fraser set about developing for the purpose of translating the Scriptures. When he encountered the Lisu people, he discovered that the whole tribe lived in fear of evil spirits that were said to inhabit the mountains. He witnessed occult rituals where devotees would practise spirit possession and cut themselves with razor-sharp swords. The people were terrified that if they did not express this perverse form of worship, they would come under a curse from the evil spirits. Fraser experienced intense spiritual warfare over his ministry among the Lisu. Moments of depression and dread would come over him as he tried to sleep at night. In the end he describes how God led a small group of people back home to begin to intercede for him and his mission. As they stood in the gap through prayer, Fraser began to experience personal breakthrough over the darkness that was trying to assault him during his time among the tribe. Nevertheless, to begin with he didn't see much fruit by way of new converts coming to Christ. On one of his sabbatical trips back home, he was reported to have been very discouraged, and said that it seemed as if the Lisu people had no need of Christ. However he persevered, and in the end they began to see a small but significant number of families come to Christ.

Fraser then set about teaching and encouraging the new converts to take responsibility for evangelizing their own people. By the time he died, there were at most a few thousand converts, but soon afterwards their numbers exploded as the Lisu Christians began to follow his example in spreading the gospel among their own people. Fraser's death has achieved almost legendary status within the Chinese Church, as the story of the old preacher from Guizhou indicates. Fraser died from cerebral malaria at fifty-two years of age. The medicine which might have saved his life he had already given to the Lisu people. Seventy-five years later, the Lisu are one of the most Christianized people groups in the whole of China with 80–90 per cent of them estimated to be Christian believers. The Religious Affairs Bureau even proposed that the official religion of the

Lisu people be changed to Christianity. They also continue to be very active in evangelism. One church we know of in Shanghai dedicated a significant amount of time and resources several years ago in helping the Lisu people build a church right at the top of a mountain. Their reasoning was that no Public Security Bureau (PSB) agents would ever be bothered enough to make the ten-hour climb to the top of a mountain in the middle of one of the remotest parts of China to cause them any trouble!

Passing on the Baton

Broadly speaking we can differentiate three categories of House Churches: The Traditional House Church, the Rural House Church, and the Urban House Church. The Traditional House Church networks that still remained after 1979 are very closely related to the first generation of church leaders who were in direct contact with the Western missionaries before 1949. Their influence is still prevalent in areas such as Shanghai, Wenzhou, Beijing, Guangzhou, and Xiamen. Leaders such as Wang Mingdao in Shanghai, Allen Yuan in Beijing, Samuel Lamb in Guangzhou, and Sister Yang Xinfei in Xiamen have made a vital contribution to the development of large networks of Traditional House Churches. These networks are the spiritual root of the modern House Church, but the suffering of the years after 1949 left a deep impression on these leaders. They learned to conduct their ministry in a very low-profile way, from which we get the term "Underground Church" of China.

Their teaching particularly emphasizes suffering for the sake of the gospel and the cultivation of one's inner spiritual life. They serve as a fundamental connection between the Western missionaries of the nineteenth and early twentieth centuries and the new era of Christianity in China.

The first wave of revival, beginning in 1979, saw the transition between the Traditional House Church and the newer Rural House Churches. Particularly in the provinces of Anhui and Henan (where Shen Xianfeng's ministry began), a large-scale commitment to nationwide evangelism that had never before been seen in China was launched. Because substantial growth had come relatively quickly, the persecution was at its fiercest in these areas. This meant that a missional culture where evangelists were sent out to all the neighbouring regions was particularly emphasized within these networks. While still technically operating "underground", the young people of this revival such as Brother Yun were highly active, as we saw in the previous chapter. The key thing to note, however, was that until 1992 this revival was almost exclusively centred around the uneducated peasant class, hence the term Rural House Church. It was not instigated or centred around any particular individual, but was a spontaneous movement of the whole community. While persecution helped the gospel to advance by forcing preachers to keep moving to new areas, it wasn't the atmosphere of persecution which opened people's hearts to the gospel. The faith of the nation in Communism was in tatters following the Cultural Revolution, and the chaotic nature of that period meant that space was afforded to the Church to grow while regular purges or attacks came from the government towards many different groups in society.

To begin with, the travelling preachers were well received in the different regions they went to, but lack of doctrinal knowledge and conflicts in church culture between the visitors and the local believers created many divisions and church splits. This led to a number of small networks being formed without any connection to the spiritual fathers of the Church. Among some of these groups, teachings and practices which ranged from the slightly bizarre to the dangerously heretical developed. In the end any group that talked about "mission" was branded as heretical by the authorities. The "Born Again" Movement led by Xu Yongze is a particular example. Because their numerical size and sphere of influence were so great, outcry for the group to be banned was heard across the nation. As a result, they were pressurized into ceasing their missionary activities within China.

In 1992, Deng Xiaoping's position as the "paramount leader" of the Chinese Communist Party had been significantly weakened in the wake of the 1989 Tian'anmen Square Massacre, when army troops had opened fire on pro-democracy student protestors in Beijing. In a final attempt to promote his reformist agenda before formally retiring from public life, Deng embarked on a southern tour of Shenzhen, Zhuhai, Guangzhou, and Shanghai. His speeches during the tour, encouraging the Chinese to "get rich", sent shockwaves throughout the whole of society that are still being felt today. In China, policy can be set through a single speech given by the person with enough influence in the Party, and this was the case in Deng's southern tour.

Suddenly, the primarily agricultural society shifted into mass urbanization. Migrant workers began to flock out of the countryside into the cities seeking their fortune. Some commentators have observed that the following twenty years in China saw the same level of societal transformation and upheaval that took 200 years to occur in the West. This dramatic shift presented a huge problem to the Rural House Churches. Up until that time, members had been actively discouraged from going into the cities, but now the vast majority of young people and preachers, who had been the lifeblood and driving force of the Rural Church, poured into the urban areas along with the rest of the rural populace. Suddenly the models of church that had been very successful in the countryside began to be put under a new kind of strain. The formerly thriving rural churches became desolate, not as a result of government oppression, but because of mass migration. This paved the way for the third category of church to develop from about the year 1999 onwards: the Urban House Church. We will spend much of the remainder of this book discussing this third type.

Watchman Nee and the Local Churches

One family of churches associated with a notable Chinese patriarch is unusual, because among the Traditional House

Church networks, it is, to my knowledge, the only one that has become a worldwide church network. Watchman Nee was one of the so-called three great fathers of the Chinese Church. The other two were Wang Mingdao, whose uncompromising refusal to submit to the Three-Self system and whose evangelical teachings have been very influential across the Chinese Church, and John Song, who despite only living to the age of forty-two saw over 100,000 Chinese come to Christ under his ministry in the 1920s and 1930s.

These three leaders were contemporaries of one another but they were each very different. Wang Mingdao was known for his defiance of the authorities, while John Song is still famous throughout East Asia for his charismatic style of ministry and the miracles of healing that would accompany his preaching. Quite a lot has already been written about him, but we learned of one previously unpublished testimony about his life and ministry from a Chinese pastor whose grandfather was a wealthy businessman in Shanghai. Whenever John Song came to the city, this pastor's grandfather would make his house available for him to stay. As a young girl, his mother noticed that John always carried around a large suitcase with him, but never seemed to wear any different clothing. One day she peered through the keyhole of John's room when he had gone to pray. She saw him open the suitcase and it was filled with pieces of paper. It turned out that, wherever he went on ministry either inside China or abroad, he would collect prayer requests from the people he met and carry them with him in his suitcase. He had a rotation system, which meant that he would work his way through his notes systematically and pray for every request he collected.

In 1920 at the age of seventeen, Watchman Nee came to Christ through the ministry of the Methodist evangelist Dora Yu. He had an extraordinary gift for assimilating information and is said to have read as many as 3,000 classic Christian writings from a wide spectrum of authors, synthesizing the revelation he received from these books into his own teaching. A British missionary by the name of Margaret E. Barber was one of the key people in his life, serving as a mentor and spiritual example to him in his twenties. In his personal testimony recorded in 1936, Nee described how the call of God began to be revealed in his life. Whenever he closed his eyes, he would see visions of local churches being birthed all over China. He viewed the key message of his life to be that God's plan is for the gospel to be revealed in the corporate body of Christ – believers united together by the Holy Spirit in their locality, not divided by doctrinal or denominational barriers. He was deeply impacted by Jesus' prayer in John 17 – that all believers may be one, even as He and the Father are one. Watchman Nee's works *The Spiritual Man* and *The Normal Christian Life* are among the most influential books on Christian life in the world, inspiring many thinkers and leaders from all kinds of different church backgrounds. The House Church family established by Watchman Nee became known in China as the "Little Flock", and elsewhere around the world as the

"Local Churches", emphasizing their strong convictions concerning the importance of the local body of Christ in a particular geographical region over trans-local networks or denominations.

When the Communists took over, Nee sensed that his ministry would come under fire, and he asked his close friend and co-worker Witness Lee to travel to Taiwan in order to ensure that the work of publishing Christian classics and planting churches could continue. By 1950, approximately 400 Local Churches had been set up through Nee's ministry in China. Witness Lee's last conversation with Watchman Nee appears to have taken place in Hong Kong that same year: he urged Nee not to return to China for fear of what might happen to him. Nee replied that if a mother discovered her house was on fire while she was outside doing the laundry, she would rush back to take care of her children no matter the danger to herself. Within two years of his return, Nee was arrested by the government, and he died in prison twenty years later. His final letter left under his pillow and written with a shaking hand read, *Christ is the Son of God who died for the redemption of sinners and resurrected after three days. This is the greatest truth in the universe. I die because of my belief in Christ. Watchman Nee.*

As Nee was taken into prison, Witness Lee was continuing their ministry in Taiwan. Churches were being planted throughout East Asia in the Philippines, Singapore, Malaysia, Thailand, and Indonesia. Within the next decade, the ministry had begun to operate in the United States, and by the mid 1970s Witness Lee had relocated their base to Anaheim in California where the organization known as Living Stream Ministry still has its headquarters today. By the 1990s, the Local Churches were spreading across North America, New Zealand, Australia, and Africa, and finally into Russia and Europe. Recently they have carried out missionary work into unreached areas such as Japan and the Middle East. Both Pastor Lee and I have spent time meeting with some of the elders and workers in Anaheim, and I have visited several Local Churches and missionaries in the UK and Europe. They estimate that there are two million Christians in Mainland China affiliated with the movement, as well as 80,000 in Taiwan, with over 250 churches now set up in the USA.

The Local Churches carry an exceptional heart of generosity towards people. In terms of the style of their meetings, they most closely resemble the Brethren. I particularly appreciate their simplicity in evangelism. They avoid arguments and debates, and their Bible studies are geared to direct encounter with God rather than doctrinal education. A good friend of mine from Taiwan once told me how he had been giving out gospel tracts on a university campus. When he offered one to a passing girl, she declined on the grounds that she was a Buddhist. My friend asked her if he could just have a few minutes to share something with her that she had never heard before. He went on to explain that all religions and philosophies, including Christianity and Buddhism, deal with the human soul. But there is a deeper place, which is the human spirit, the part of us that was created to be in communion with God. Jesus' sacrifice on the cross was so that God's Spirit could be united again with His children, not to get people to follow a particular religion. The girl was intrigued; however, she countered once again that she was a Buddhist. He then replied quite simply, *That's fine – stay being a Buddhist if you like. Just make sure you get Christ into your spirit!* He understood that it is God who brings about a change in the human heart, and that can only happen from within. The task of mission is not about exporting a culture, philosophy, or religious system, it is introducing people to a Person. In taking this approach, they sidestep many of the arguments and pitfalls that are often present as obstacles to people accepting the gospel.

The New Shape of the Church

One of the key characteristics of the Traditional and Rural Chinese House Churches is that while their roots go back to spiritual fathers and mothers who came from a mixture of theological and denominational backgrounds, the first few decades during which they were beginning to form their unique identity took place in almost complete isolation from the International Church. The Chinese Church continued to be centred around small groups of people seeking to live out their faith together in community. It was not possible for large-scale Sunday meetings, in which the ordained few minister to the many, to become the status quo. Spiritual passivity was not an option! This is important to note as we start to look in the next chapter at the development of the Urban House Church.

What does this shape of church have to say to us in the West? To answer that question, I would like to borrow the language of the ministry of Watchman Nee, one of the few Chinese leaders who has been a spiritual father to both East and West. God's plan is for individual Christian's relationship with Christ to grow into a corporate expression of that relationship. From there, we are supposed to grow up into a place of habitation for His presence, what the Scripture calls the temple of the Holy Spirit (Ephesians 2:21; 1 Corinthians 3:16). This is where people who don't know Him are able to encounter Him, just as they could in the Temple at Jerusalem in the Old Testament. If you want to meet God you need to go to the place where He lives, which is in His people. From the temple, God wants us to grow into the city, which is referred to in the book of Revelation as the New Jerusalem. The city phase is where the Church is mature enough to spread throughout all spheres of society, becoming salt that stops corruption and light that dispels darkness (Matthew 5:14). Finally, the reign of God – or God's kingdom – is allowed to manifest.

The problem many of us face in the West is that we stumble over the very first stage, the point at which our individual relationship with Christ is supposed to mature into our corporate relationship with Him. Because many Christians are stuck as passive recipients of teaching and ministry, having a "meeting-driven" Christianity rather than one that puts equal emphasis on knowing Christ in every aspect of life, we end up with a "special" minority who are really able to be fully functional in their spiritual life and a majority who are stuck at different stages of immaturity. Then we try to skip ahead to be the city of God through different evangelistic or social activities aimed at reaching society, but we haven't first learned to become the body of Christ or the temple of His presence, so we find that many of our programmes and activities are quite shallow and powerless. The secular world then sees this as hypocrisy and doesn't want anything to do with the Church. God's kingdom is all about relationships: our relationship with God and with one another. When we adopt a model of spiritual fatherhood that is based on hierarchy and religious system rather than on relationship, our identity becomes confused and the Church is unable to grow up fully into the headship of Christ.

If there is one lesson for us to learn from the way God has moved in China, I believe it is that now is the time for us to re-examine the way we operate in Western Christianity. Do we really know how to love one another as Christ loved us? Are we really seeking to be one even as Christ and the Father are one? The unique environment of twentieth-century China has caused these values to be deeply ingrained in the spiritual DNA of the House Churches, and it is one of the many things that they have to offer the International Church in the twenty-first century.

The Urban House Church

The sudden rise of the Urban House Churches is a turning point in the history of China's House Churches.

Dr Ezra Jin, Pastor, Beijing Zion Church

The Not-so-hidden Kingdom

So far we have looked at the spiritual foundations of the Chinese Church as well as the first major phase of revival, which took place hidden *behind the walls* of a closed nation. Looking back to 2 Chronicles 14:7, the next phase in building the towns was to raise up the towers:

> *"Let us build up these towns," he said to Judah, "and put **walls** around them, with **towers**, gates and bars..."*

If the Church started out developing predominantly in secret during the *wall* phase, the shift in focus from the rural regions to the cities prepared the way for an expression of church that is far more high profile. This shift had brought a change in the dynamics between Church and state. For instance in Wuhan, an Urban House Church was holding their weekly meeting in a hotel conference suite overlooking Shouyi Square where anti-Japanese protests were taking place over the disputed Diaoyu islands in the East China Sea. At least ten other House Churches from different networks all meet in that same office block. Although the government maintains tight controls across the whole of society, the Chinese people are no stranger to demonstrations. In fact tens of thousands are taking place across the country every year. As it happened, the police unit assigned to monitor Shouyi Square decided to set up their temporary base of operations in the very same hotel. The PSB headquarters for Wuhan is just around the corner. While they were moving in with their equipment, the officers in charge became aware of the loud music and singing coming from the nearby conference facilities. When they went over to tell the pastor to break up the meeting and stop making noise, he replied that they still had another half an hour of praise and worship to go before they finished, and in any case the church was there first so the police would just have to wait!

Fifteen years ago it would have been unthinkable that such an exchange could have taken place. We are more used to stories from China of pastors being thrown into prison and Bibles smuggled across the border in the middle of the night than such public and open demonstrations of faith. This is just one of the considerable changes that have taken place in China over the last few years. By way of further illustration, one House Church leader we know was recently brought in by the police for questioning. When they let him leave after a few hours they told him that he was lucky it was not ten years ago, otherwise he would certainly have been violently interrogated.

From the Countryside to the Cities

The Rural House Church revival of the 1980s was built on the hidden foundations of an underground movement, but the start of mass migration from the rural regions to the cities fuelled by China's economic boom paved the way for the Church to enter its next phase. Previously, most Chinese believers were from a rural, uneducated background, meaning that their social standing and thus their influence on a governmental or political level was very limited. By the early 2000s, a new style of church was emerging, led by believers from a completely different social demographic. This next generation of church pastors started holding meetings in offices, factories, restaurants, or conference centres without any attempt to conceal what they were doing from the authorities. Generally referred to as the Urban House Churches, these are still technically illegal as they do not subscribe to the Three-Self system, but they don't operate in an "underground" or hidden manner as is typical of the Rural House Church. They represent the towers rising above the walls.

One of the key changes that has allowed for the rise of the Urban House Church has been the emergence of leaders from among the intellectual classes. For the last twenty years, more and more academics, entrepreneurs, journalists, and even politicians have been taking a strong interest in Christianity. It seems that the more China has grown economically, the more obviously the spiritual vacuum at the heart of the nation has become apparent, and many people who come from places of influence and privilege have become hungry for God. At a time when the whole of Chinese society is facing an identity crisis, the Christian gospel is offering a credible alternative to Confucianism and Communism alike.

A word that is now often to be heard in Urban House Church circles is a significant one: *kingdom*. Whereas the Traditional and Rural House Church networks have classically emphasized a salvation message that is characterized by perseverance through suffering, this new generation is by comparison profoundly optimistic about society. They are contending for social reformation in many different spheres, and they are not afraid to engage directly with the authorities. They have a kingdom theology that expects to see the life and power of Christ demonstrated in such a way that it disciples and transforms an entire nation. For most of the older generation of House Church leaders, their relationship with the state has been a very difficult one. Their world was simple and roles were clearly defined. The Communist regime represented the enemy who was trying to persecute and destroy the Church, and their hope for societal transformation was set fully on the return of Christ. The idea of forming any kind of partnership with the state would be totally unthinkable to them, neither did they have a theology which included the reformation of society.

This is partly why many leaders refused to join the Three-Self movement, to the extent that many suffered long years in prison as a result. It was not so much that they denied the authenticity of the Three-Self believers' faith, as it was an ideological and theological division. The TSPM movement is headed by a secular state, but the Church is supposed to be headed by Christ. Even if the Chinese government had been more relaxed and open towards the Church in the early days, I suspect that many of the same House Church leaders would still have struggled with giving over church governance to an irreligious institution. There has never been anything like the established Roman Catholic or Anglican churches in China where the Church was integrated with society and politics. It was a time when things were very polarized: countryside and city, House Church and Three-Self, the hidden kingdom of God versus the government of man. Actively engaging in the sociopolitical world was totally off the cards for the Rural House Churches even if there had been the opportunity to do so. For a time, key leaders like Shen Xianfeng would even actively discourage their members from moving to the cities for fear that their spiritual life would be adversely affected. It wasn't until the mid to late 1990s that they understood the mass migration out of the rural areas to be something instigated by God which they should work with, rather than against. It was after this period that networks such as the Chinese Gospel Fellowship began actively planting churches in the cities.

At first the Rural House Church networks that did decide to engage in the cities tried to use the same model of church that they were used to seeing in the countryside. Their main aim was pastoral: to cater for Christian migrant workers who had been converted in the 1980s and early 1990s, or young people who were second-generation believers and had moved into the cities to study or find work. They quickly learned that the social divisions between the rural peasant class and the urban intellectual class meant that these fellowships found it hard to engage with the city. The simple, basic message of the Rural House Church was unable to meet the needs of a rapidly evolving culture. The spiritual need is the same, but the context is different. The rural believers were poor, perhaps only having a single plate of fruit to share between twenty or thirty people in a fellowship meeting, but they would always make sure there was something left over to give to the homeless and destitute afterwards. Today the average cost of an apartment in central Shanghai is more than in central London! The young generation in China's cities have grown up in a time of massive liberalization and economic boom. They are faced with thousands of options and life choices that did not exist twenty years ago, and they have a need for a kind of church that is able to speak to the issues that are relevant to them. The church in Wuhan that is pastored by Shen Xianfeng has radically shifted its approach in order to reach this new generation. They meet on the top floor of a modern shopping mall called Genesis (named presumably after the Biblical reference, even though the mall's owner is not known to be a Christian), and include meetings with a worship band, digital projectors, and PA systems. They share their premises with another Urban House Church, which uses it to run a theological training college.

New Leaders for a New Season

Some pastors such as Ezra Jin began their ministry in the Three-Self Church before leaving to start Urban House Churches. Their encounter with the gospel did not come through direct contact with the revivals in the countryside, nor did it come through connections overseas. The separation in social class between the peasants and the city-dwellers meant that it would be fairly unusual for a person from China's educated elite to have any contact with a rural evangelist – unless it was through family connections. For Pastor Jin, one of the key turning points for this generation was the Tian'anmen Square incident of 1989, known to many Chinese simply as 4 June. He recalls the lively discussions in the student body and among the lecturing staff all about democratic freedom and the future of Chinese society when he was a student at Beijing University. They saw the Communist Party as having become the main force hindering China's development. These discussions had a deep effect on Jin, causing him to lose his faith in the Party and abandon his ambitions for a career within its ranks.

I first started to go to church in 1987, he says. *It was Chongwen Church, part of the Three-Self movement. [In fact the Three-Self churches were also experiencing a massive growth in numbers at that time as a kind of overflow effect from the Rural House Church revival.] Most of the people in the church were elderly, and I didn't really understand what the pastor was talking about. Christianity seemed to me to be a very passive religion. If all the young people were to become Christians, then who would take responsibility for the future of the nation? It wasn't that I had any kind of a Christian upbringing which prompted me to go to church. My parents were typical peasants who had no connection to Christianity. I went because I was searching for what the true meaning of life was.*

The real turning point for me came after the June 4th incident. What happened on that day has forever become a part of me. I was in my third year at university. Like many other students, I wasn't much of an activist myself, but I supported and agreed with student activism and had taken part in various demonstrations on a number of occasions. On June 3rd and 4th I wasn't in Beijing; I had gone to Qingdao because of some family business. I remember it all so clearly. On the morning of the 4th I had climbed to the top of Mt Tai to watch the sunrise. When I reached the bottom, I suddenly heard a high-pitched siren and an American broadcast saying that the army had opened fire on the students in Beijing. It was a unique moment – hearing that American voice through the wailing siren. When I understood what had happened it felt as if the whole world had collapsed around me. I decided to immediately return to Beijing.

From 21 April 1989, approximately 100,000 students had become involved in demonstrations in the huge Tian'anmen Square in China's capital city. In the early hours of the morning of 4 June, they suddenly found themselves surrounded by tanks accompanied by soldiers in their hundreds of thousands. Residents of the city had attempted to block the advance of the army on the square, but some of the tanks had made use of a honeycomb of underground tunnels that had been built under the city as a transport network and bomb shelter in the event of a nuclear strike. It would have seemed as if these vehicles appeared out of nowhere as they drove into the square from the tunnels. A friend of mine from the United States was out on a short-term mission trip in China at the time. Several days before the army moved in he had been in the square sharing the gospel with some of the students. On the day of the incident he had only just travelled up to a university in Manchuria when he heard the same American broadcast described by Pastor Jin come through the radio. He said that the students he spoke to were completely bewildered. They couldn't believe that their own government had opened fire on their fellow students. Shortly afterwards, they received word that the army was moving in on his location, and he was air-evacuated out of the country via Hong Kong.

For many students, the event was just as Jin had described. It was as if their world had ended:

> *I arrived back in Beijing early on June 5th. The whole city was paralysed, totally different from just a few days before. There were no buses and people were scattering out of the city. Back at the university, all the teachers were advising us to get home as soon as possible. They suspected that the military was about to take over the school and initiate martial law. They could at any moment begin arresting students at random and it wouldn't be safe to stay, so I packed up my things as best I could, struggling to hold back the tears. My whole being was shrouded in a thick hopelessness. The world that I knew had been completely shattered.*

In the aftermath of the deaths of his classmates and the shattered illusions of his country, Jin carried on life in a daze, numb and detached. Not long after returning back to the university, he met one of the friends he had made from Chongwen Church. She told him that one old lady who had taken a particular interest in his explorations of the Christian faith had passed away from liver cancer. He was told that to her very last she was praying for him to come to know Christ.

> *When I heard that piece of news it struck a deep chord within me,* he said. *Students in the 1980s in China had no freedom and no independence. Very few of us knew what it was to be loved. Everything was provided for by government grants, even our toothbrushes and toothpaste. We were an abstract entity – people of the state. After June 4th I suddenly felt as if I had been abandoned, rejected, and deceived. Under such immense pressure I found myself suffocating, unable to speak about it. Neither could I bring myself to watch the news reports from the authorities any longer. Even after more than 20 years I still don't watch the news. Back then, hearing of how that old lady had such a care and concern for me moved me in a profound way.*

The funeral for this old lady turned out to be a major step on Jin's journey to faith. In the villages as a young boy he had been puzzled by Christian funerals. There had been no offerings of incense made for the dead or kow-towing to the spirits of the ancestors. The church members would even sing songs around the grave. To a traditional Chinese mindset this would be seen as highly disrespectful and a violation of the teachings of Confucius, which were the underpinning of traditional Chinese society. This time, however, something about the way the church came together to celebrate the life of a simple old lady touched him deeply. As he saw the congregation gather around and heard them singing a Chinese hymn entitled *Crossing the Jordan to see the Father's Face*, he felt a change of heart. Faith in Christ no longer appeared to be a form of escapism. The hope that they were celebrating in the midst of loss was a stark contrast to the hopelessness expressed at the traditional Chinese funerals he had attended. Suddenly faith was a courageous thing, and he admired them for it. Prior to that moment, he hadn't been able to understand the way the Christians had spoken about life and death and their hope in Christ. Now he had experienced the power of that hope first hand:

> *I discovered an unwavering hope within their singing that ordinary people do not have,* he said. *It caused me to recall the words of the existentialist philosopher Kierkegaard I had once read: "Having faith requires us to pay a price, but to have no faith requires an even greater price." I realized in that moment that one loses hope when there is no basis for hope. I hadn't been able to understand the Bible until then. I had been*

*certain that God didn't exist, but after attending
that funeral I realized just how important God's
existence really is.*

From then on, Jin became a very active member of the church. He eagerly listened throughout the lengthy sermons that had previously been so difficult to understand and frequented a small Bible study with a group of older believers. Because their short-term memory had weakened with age, they would often forget what had been studied the previous week and so would have to start their readings all over again from the beginning every time, but Jin continued to take notes and study along with them. He found himself spending much of his time helping out wherever he could in the church, even cleaning the toilets. After several months, he had made quite an impression on the congregation, especially as he was the only student from the prestigious Beijing University who had ever attended. At that time very few university students went to church. Despite his active involvement in the church, Jin's big questions still remained unanswered. Instead of focusing on his fast-approaching final examinations, his mind kept turning them over: *Does God really exist? Who am I? Why am I here?* His classmates tried to persuade him to spend less time at church. A degree from Beijing University is a sure guarantee of future employment, and they were worried that he was getting too caught up in religion to pass.

Then finally an American university student from University of California, Berkeley, who was in the church on short-term mission suddenly challenged him one day. *Do you want to become a real Christian?* he said. Jin's reply was indignant, *Are you trying to say that I'm a fake Christian?* When he saw the expression on Jin's face, the American student pushed further:

> *Going to church, studying the Bible, and doing church ministry don't make a person into a real Christian. Real Christianity is a personal connection that Jesus makes with your life. If you know that you have a need in your heart, then knock on the door and ask the Lord to open your heart to Him. He will come in and make Himself known to you.*

An inexplicable force behind these words sent a shock right through Jin. For the first time he realized that he was a person who needed God's salvation:

> *As I knelt on the floor to pray, I truly experienced the presence of God. I asked Jesus to come into my life and be my Lord. Although my eyes were filled with tears, a great elation was in my heart. Once the meeting had ended I made the 40-minute cycle ride back to Beijing University. Such an unspeakable joy was all over me – a joy that no one could take away. It was like a long-lost child who had been kidnapped from his family finally returning home, his father waiting expectantly at the door. All the injustices and the bitter tears*

*are washed away in that instant when the father
stretches out his arms to embrace him. That was
the day I was born again.*

Since the Tian'anmen Square incident, the whole student
body had been plunged into a fog of hopelessness. After
his encounter with the presence of God at the church
meeting, a wholly new appreciation for life found Jin. On
returning to his student dormitory, he found all of his
classmates playing cards. Playing cards or the traditional
gambling game mah-jong had become the one act of
defiance against the government left to them. One of his
friends taunted him as he came in, *Hey Jin, did God speak
to you today?* In a loud voice, Jin replied boldly, *Yes God did
indeed speak to me!*

In that moment, a baptism of the love of Christ came
over him. He was gripped with a sudden desire to do
something to bless all his friends who were sitting there,
life ticking over day after day. He began boiling kettles of
water to take to all the students in the three neighbouring
dormitories for them to drink. Chinese people tend not
to drink cold water, and the issue over boiled water was
quite contentious in the dormitories. None of the students
ever wanted to make the effort to go and boil water for
themselves, so they would habitually take boiled water
from others without asking. It was unheard of for anyone
just to prepare any for someone else! After this, the attitude
among that group changed towards the Church. They
started saying that going to church could genuinely turn

someone into a better person. Jin, however, is very clear. The thing that changed him was not the Church, but the comfort and the love of God in Jesus.

A Message of Hope

Ezra Jin began his ministry as a preacher in the Three-Self Church. During every meeting, several government agents would be present at the back to monitor what was going on. At that time there were many restrictions on what the Church could or could not preach, but Jin was known for pushing the boundaries in terms of the content of his messages. He commented that he treated every sermon as if it would be his last, but each time the authorities left without causing him any trouble. After spending four years at theological college abroad, he eventually returned to Beijing to set up Zion Church in 2007, an Urban House Church which exists outside the Three-Self system. The Chinese-speaking congregation began with just seven people meeting in a room, while a few more than twenty missionaries made up a Korean-speaking congregation. Another church of thirty or forty members, which was seeking a pastor, decided to join them, and within a year they had seen the church grow to over 300. By the end of the second year, this doubled to around 600. Jin took the decision to limit the number of members in order not to expand beyond the capabilities of the leadership, and they have subsequently planted several other congregations in the city as well as sending church planters to other regions of China, including Lanzhou and Yunnan. A high percentage of the congregation is university educated, from a professional background, and most of them are under forty years old. Their monthly rent for the building they use for meetings and a theological college is 100,000 yuan, equivalent to £10,000. Part of their ministry includes a legal team who have been campaigning for a change in the law that would allow churches like Zion to have an official, legal identity.

Jin has worked hard to build bridges with the government authorities because he believes that it is time for the salt and light of the kingdom to bring transformation to China on every level. The Scripture says *a city on a hill cannot be hidden*, so for the Urban House Churches continuing to operate "underground" is not an option. Many people in China feel they have been left with nothing but money and the pursuit of money. Value in relationships, family, and spirituality has reached an all-time low. In recent years, there has been a strong rise in interest in spiritual matters, and these new, highly visible expressions of church are seeking to broadcast God's hope into a hopeless world. I feel that Jin himself sums things up very well in the conclusion of his own testimony of how he came to Christ:

> *On that day in the student dormitories, I saw that those students sitting around were all the cream of the crop in China. Yet they were so void of hope. Was there any true peace that could come through*

sitting around playing cards? Heaven and hell are laid out together in the same world. Those without Jesus are submerged in hopelessness, and that was exactly my experience before knowing Him! I have an intimate knowledge of what it means to be without hope. Now, whenever I preach, the word I use more than anything else is "hope". Only one who has come out of a life of hopelessness can truly understand how beautiful a life of hope really is.

God's Lighthouses

If we cannot register with the authorities, then we will register in the hearts of the people.

Pastor Huang, Wuhan

Establishing the Gates

... Put walls around them, with towers and **gates**.

(2 Chronicles 14:7)

The grace of God that is contained within the tower is useless to the world unless there is a way and a means for it to flow out to society. In Ezekiel's vision of the river of God flowing from the temple, the ultimate goal of the river was to enter the Dead Sea and bring life to its waters (Ezekiel 47). Referring back to the testimony of Mrs He Enzheng from chapter 1, the prophetic word given to the early pioneers of the Chinese mission movement concerned the Chinese Church becoming releasers of God's grace, and not merely receivers. Jesus told His disciples *freely you have received, now freely give* (Matthew 10:8). God's intention in building His Church is always that it will be a conduit of His grace and blessing to a dying world. A view that restricts the role of the Chinese Church to being simply passive receivers of foreign missions denies God's kingdom purpose in the revival sweeping China. Napoleon famously predicted China's impact on the world when he said, *Let China sleep, for when she wakes she will shake the whole world*. As situations have arisen that have shaken China, the Church has been stepping up to its missionary calling. At least as early as the SARS epidemic in 2002, the Church has demonstrated the extent of its ability to mobilize and release believers for mission. Up until this point, the House Churches of Beijing had not been given the opportunity for any large-scale, public evangelism. However, when the government declared a state of national emergency, many of the Christians remained in the capital city while a mass exodus of those rich enough to afford the time away from work was taking place. These believers took the opportunity to take to the streets in open evangelistic activity, giving out tracts, preaching the gospel across the city, and worshipping openly without fear of reprisals.

The most significant turning point in the relationship between the House Churches and the Chinese government was the Wenchuan Earthquake of 2008. Nearly 90,000 people were pronounced dead or missing, and over 350,000 were left injured. The devastation that swept through the region shocked the entire nation. In the run-up to the Beijing Olympics, the optimism and national pride of Chinese society was brought crashing down to the cold, hard reality of man's inability to truly master his own destiny. Thousands of volunteer aid workers came flooding in from across China to help in the aftermath, with the relief effort managed by various disaster-response teams under the direction of the Chinese government. It soon became apparent, however, that about 60-70 per cent of all the aid workers had come from China's House Churches, both rural and urban. Until then, no one had been fully aware of the scale on which the House Churches of China were able to operate. Moreover, the government agencies commented that their organization and effectiveness while working in the disaster zone rivalled that of the government's own teams, and in some cases was even considered to be of a higher quality. Whole congregations relocated from different parts of the country to plant right in the centre of the worst-hit areas to serve the people there in any way they could.

There was a Christian woman living in a small town in the earthquake zone. Several days before the earthquake happened, she felt impressed by the Holy Spirit to stockpile food and some living essentials to prepare for a natural disaster that was about to hit. She shared the news with some of the other believers in the area, and after they prayed together to seek further confirmation they all agreed with what she sensed. When they tried to inform the townspeople, they laughed at them and took no notice. The earthquake caused a landslide, which completely cut the town off from the outside world. It was many days before the relief teams were able to unblock the roads to get any aid into the area, but God was so concerned about this town that He led his people to stockpile food for them so that they would be safe during the disaster. When people came to share the gospel with the townspeople in the aftermath, 98 per cent decided to become Christians as a result. Prior to this, the whole village were traditional idol-worshipping families.

Until then, there had never been such a great opportunity for the Chinese Church to publicly demonstrate that rather than being an enemy of social stability, the body of Christ is the greatest conduit for blessing and social prosperity a nation could hope for. Proverbs 11:11 states, *By the blessing of the righteous the city is exalted, but by the mouth of the wicked it is torn down.* As the Chinese Church has spread into more and more spheres of society, gateways are being opened to allow the grace of God invested in it to be released into China at large. The towers that have been raised up to be so visible in Chinese society are now shining as beacons of light and hope. God has always desired a people who understand how to carry His life and fullness as *treasure in jars of clay* to a world that is far from Him. It would be easy to become embittered and critical towards the Chinese government, especially with such a history of persecution towards the Church, but Chinese believers are beginning to understand what it means to light a candle instead of cursing the darkness. At this stage more than ever, it is vital for the Church to continue to return good even for evil. We have no authority to pray for or speak into the life of people over whom we presume to stand in judgment or criticism.

Social Action

Brother Meng is the director of the Holy Love Foundation, one of the oldest charitable organizations in China. It was established in 1994. Several years ago, Meng's family were forced to escape to another country in East Asia because a local organized crime group had been trying to intimidate them into giving over the large plot of land and building complex that had been set up as a home and school for disabled children. Until the Urban House Church days, many leaders were reluctant to get involved in social action projects that were not directly evangelistic. Even when the earthquake happened, there were still churches that felt it wasn't their place to do anything about it. Meng's view is simple: two-thirds of Jesus' ministry in the Bible was about action, while one-third was about preaching and teaching. When the Wenchuan Earthquake hit on 12 May 2008, he immediately asked his wife to organize a rescue team from among the Christians that they were in contact with. The strategy was twofold: to reveal God's glory through demonstrating His love to society in the midst of crisis, and to show the government that the Christian Church is a blessing and not a threat. As a member of the International Red Cross, Meng was positioned as the key person for the House Churches to liaise with the authorities during the crisis. In fact 95 per cent of the official passes that were issued to Christian volunteers in the relief effort were arranged by him. His ministry is a prophetic sign to the wider Chinese Church that they must engage with the needs of the world around them, allowing the heart of Christ's love for people to be at the centre of all that they do.

Inspired by the example of this kind of ministry, an Urban House Church pastor in Wuhan called Huang founded the Wuhan Shouyi Agape Foodbank in 2010. In the run-up to the grand opening, they received a communication from the local authorities that they were not allowed to have any publicity or large celebration to advertise the food bank. One day before the launch another message came through, this time from the American consulate in Wuhan. Somehow the consulate had learned that this new charity was about to open, and they asked if they could send an official delegation to the opening. Naturally the church was more than happy to welcome the American diplomats, and once the consulate became involved, it would be an extreme loss of face for the local Chinese authorities to not also show their support. As a result, they hastily changed their position and organized an official delegation to come and openly support the charity. It then so happened that on the day of the launch, the consulate arranged for four international media organizations to come with them and provide news coverage of the event! God has His ways of getting the message out.

The food bank has now been able to register with the local Bureau for Industry and Commerce, and is recruiting volunteers from across a wide spectrum of society. Although it has been set up as a Christian organization, people of all faiths and none are able to take part in the distribution of food packages to the poor. Their system involves identifying families who are most in need of support, and they will provide packages for as long as is needed until the recipients are able to support themselves. The next stage of their plans is to set up an employment service, which is able to train people in the skills that they need to work.

Open Evangelism

In meeting with Urban House Church leaders, we have found that all of them feel that part of God's purpose in raising up their churches is to cause Christianity to become highly visible and actively engaged in society. In major cities such as Shanghai, Hangzhou, and Wuhan, many Urban House Churches are leading the way in carrying out regular, open-air evangelism. They find that public and Christian holidays are a great opportunity to go out onto the streets and share the gospel with people.

For Chinese New Year, believers in one town in central China came out and held a traditional Spring Festival procession. The only difference was that instead of the traditional songs and decorations, they came out singing hymns and carrying banners with evangelistic one-liners and Scriptures. They openly shared the message with people that Jesus loves them, and handed out invitations to celebration meetings hosted by the church.

Not all of these events go smoothly, however. One church in Shenzhen had hundreds of people come for a Christmas gathering at the end of 2012. They had booked a hotel conference suite and prepared to host a traditional Christmas celebration service where the church members could invite their friends to come and hear a gospel message. To begin with, it seemed that the meeting went without a hitch, but either government agents had come in as spies or else someone in the meeting contacted the authorities. Although these meetings are carried out very openly, they are still technically illegal! As a consequence, the young pastor of the church was subsequently arrested and put in prison overnight as a punishment. The hotel was actually owned by a member of the church, and the pastor deliberately took full responsibility for the whole meeting so as to protect him.

Although more and more Urban House Churches are experimenting with large-scale evangelistic meetings, the main form of outreach is much more focused on one-to-one contact. Most of the growth in the Urban House Churches actually comes through personal or friendship evangelism, much the same as it is now in the Western Church.

One of the biggest mission fields targeted by the Urban House Churches is the university campuses. They recognize that if they are going to see reformation come to the nation, they have to reach the future movers and shakers who are filling China's centres of higher education. University places are fiercely competitive, and unless a person becomes a successful entrepreneur, pursuing education has become the most important means of social mobility in the country. It is now quite common to find Christian students running small group Bible studies in their dormitories, and reaching many of their friends for Christ in this way. More and more students and professionals are willing to openly profess their Christian identity without fear of negative reprisals.

Help from the West

For many believers and leaders in the Urban House Churches, contact with Western believers has been crucial in their journey to faith. For the last two decades, new opportunities have arisen for a wave of students to leave the country and study abroad. These had spent their formative years not in the insane fires of the Cultural Revolution, but in the "open door" China of the 1980s onwards. Coming from an institutionally atheist education system but lacking the commitment to Communist ideology held by their parents' generation, many people began to embrace the moral and ethical framework of Christianity through their personal reading of Christian history and theology. Others, such as Ezra Jin (discussed in Chapter 4), found that the disillusionment caused by the Tian'anmen Square incident left them hungry for spiritual answers. Many academics became what we refer to as "cultural Christians" – that is to say they seek to adopt a Christian ethic without necessarily a strong commitment to Christ. It is often when these cultural Christians encounter believers with a real, intrinsic faith that they find a personal relationship with Christ themselves.

Among the academic community in China today, there is now an informal network of Christian academics and university lecturers which connects people nationally for fellowship and mutual support. It was founded by a university professor from Shanghai who is an expert in Old Testament theology. His was a typical story of a cultural Christian finding real faith abroad. It was when he came to England on an academic exchange that he first heard the gospel in a Bible study led by Pastor Lee. He was struck by the revelation that he could into a real relationship with God rather than just a set of teachings on how someone should live their life. Shortly afterwards, he made a personal commitment to Christ and was baptized. After he returned to Shanghai, he was struck by the need for a stronger Christian presence in Chinese universities, so he began to work through his contacts to set up the network. His efforts came to the attention of the Party officials in the university who warned him that he would get into trouble since the network amounted to an illegal religious organization. Choosing to follow his own conviction, the professor decided that he would take the risk and set up the network regardless. So far he hasn't had any further problems with the authorities.

House Church Sunday School using a Three-Self building.

A House Church Sunday School. Sunday Schools are common in the West, but in China it is a risk to outreach to children as under eighteen-year-olds are prohibited from being "proselytized".

BTJ early pioneer, Mrs He Enzheng (see pp. 16 and 147).

CHC leaders' training.

House Church Bible
Study Group praise
and worship.

Prayer rooms
such as this
are very
common in
CHC places
of worship.

Evangelism in the market place. These two cafés reach out to customers (see p. 168).

The Teddy Beloved café shares the gospel and leads customers to Christ (see p. 168).

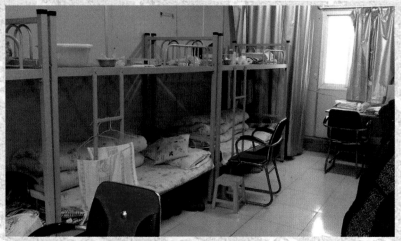

The Aixin Healing Centre provides food and lodging for patients. The facilities are basic, but guests are cared for and prayed over for two weeks to receive healing (see pp. 106–109).

This building under construction was purpose-built for the church to have a bigger and better worship space by a couple who received miraculous blessing from the Lord.

Rural House Church worshipping in subzero temperatures with their hearts burning for the Kingdom.

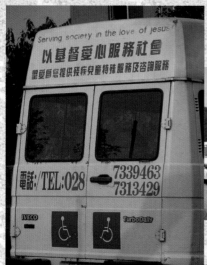

Providing disaster relief after the Wenchuan earthquake (see p. 89).

Food aid in the earthquake zone – social service with the love of Jesus (see p. 89).

This special school run by the Chinese House Church caters for disadvantaged and disabled children (see p. 91).

Training Centres.

Urban House Church.

Urban House Church modern worship venue in an office block (see p. 71).

Urban House Church worship in a hotel conference room (see p. 71).

Prayer and intercession in the desert, before and after the miraculous spring burst up from the ground (see p. 136).

Xi'an to Zion, the vision of an arrow in Kashgar (see p. 147).

Many among this new generation of university-educated Chinese have been baptized while studying abroad in Europe or the United States. While I was a postgraduate student at the University of Bath, the husband of one of my classmates came to visit her from China. While in England, his wife had joined a local Chinese Christian fellowship and had made a personal commitment to Christ. When her husband Tony arrived, he confessed to harbouring a growing spiritual hunger to know God. After spending an afternoon discussing the Bible, I had the privilege of praying with him to give his life to Christ, and after returning to Beijing he joined an Urban House Church. Quite a stir was caused by his conversion to Christianity, as in order to join the Communist Party he had originally been obliged to sign a document renouncing any religious faith. His supervisor at the university angrily reminded him that he could not be a Party member and a Christian, to which he replied that he saw no contradiction between the two. In his eyes, following Christ enabled him to better serve his country and didn't restrict his involvement in the academic and political worlds. In the end, the university supported his request to completely change the focus of his doctoral research and began to fund his investigation into the growing influence of the House Churches on Chinese society!

Pastor Lee has for many years been involved in ministering to overseas Chinese who have come to the UK for work or study. On one occasion, a Chinese PhD student in Oxford stumbled across the Chinese fellowship where he was ministering. This student had been out cycling one day when he was in China and had passed by a Three-Self Church. Intrigued by the sound of the hymns, he decided to go in and find out what was going on. He was so moved by the peace of God during the meeting that he decided to accept Jesus without anyone even talking to him. After he came to the UK and had joined the Chinese Bible study group in Oxford with his wife, he decided that he wanted to get baptized. Pastor Lee asked him if he wanted a public or private baptism in case there might be some trouble from the Chinese authorities. He said that since he'd dedicated his life to Christ, he would prefer to have a public ceremony rather than a private one. The week before he was baptized, he was away in another city in England for an academic conference. Another delegate who had come from China asked him if he knew of a Chinese citizen who was going to be baptized in Oxford, not knowing that it was the very man himself. It turns out that the Chinese authorities had been spying on him the whole time! He was quite shaken by the experience, but after praying it through he decided that he would still go ahead with the public baptism.

His wife meanwhile had still not received Christ for herself even though she was regularly having personal Bible studies with the pastor. One day her husband came home from his lab at the university to find that his wife was a completely changed person. He had never before seen her so cheerful. He was immediately worried that he might have forgotten it was her birthday or their wedding anniversary, but in fact she told him that while she was preparing a meal in the kitchen annexe at the back of their house that afternoon, she suddenly saw Jesus physically walk through the back garden towards her. *Follow me*, He said. Immediately she fell to her knees and gave her life to Him. For such a highly sceptical woman to have an encounter like this left a deep impression on the church community. After such a radical paradigm shift, this couple found that God was calling them into ministry. They are now serving as church leaders in Canada.

When Chinese people become Christians, they desperately want to bring their families to Him as well. Their background under the Communist Party means that they understand from a very young age what it means to dedicate oneself completely to a higher cause. When they come to Christ, that same dedication is redirected towards God and His kingdom. There is a sense of responsibility that goes beyond the individual, into the family and wider society.

God is reaching thousands of Chinese students in the West. Never before in the history of China has such a high number of Chinese come to live and study abroad. Of those who stay, many, if not most, end up becoming Christians. They harbour an innate curiosity towards Christianity viewing it as foundational to Western culture if nothing else. In our interview with Ezra Jin, he emphasized the way in which the present move of God in China cannot be separated from the prayers and service of Western believers from 200 years ago. In those days cross-cultural mission was an incredibly difficult and dangerous affair. Today many of the churches of Europe and America don't even need to buy a plane ticket to participate in cross-cultural mission. With the increasing size of immigrant communities, they need only open up the doors and step outside to meet those of another culture. Chinese people in the West are particularly open to exploring questions of faith. I think it has something to do with the huge amount of prayer that has been saturating the country for many years, both from inside and outside its borders. We believe that God has a plan to use these overseas Chinese believers to have a substantial impact on the Western Church, just as the Church has had an impact upon them.

Reaching the Chinese to Reach Europe

Several ministries have arisen in Europe specifically aimed at reaching the vast number of Chinese students and immigrants that have been coming over the last fifteen years or so. Just as China is rising as a superpower with increasing levels of global influence, so too does the Chinese Church have a worldwide calling. Pastor Lee's own organization, Love China International, has been one of the major instruments for revival among the Chinese communities of Europe. Historically, the Christians of these communities have been very conservative in their theology and style of worship. One of the key elements of Love China International's ministry has been to introduce these churches to the Holy Spirit and promote spiritual renewal among them, as well as establish strong partnerships between Western and Eastern churches. Since 2002, Pastor Lee has made regular trips into Europe to preach in the Cantonese- and Mandarin-speaking communities, and host the Europe-wide Life Impact Conference for Chinese believers. Out of that first trip alone, three people are now in ministry in different cities in Mainland China, and one has continued to serve God as a missionary to Germany.

Many of those who have been saved or baptized in the Holy Spirit through the Life Impact Conference have gone on to plant churches or lead ministries around the world. This new generation of Chinese pastors and missionaries is going to become instrumental in helping to build an international platform for the Chinese Church to enter fully into worldwide missions, a vision commonly referred to as "Back to Jerusalem". Most of the newly ordained Chinese Church leaders in Paris for instance have received their calling to ministry through the Life Impact Conference. As God begins to move again powerfully across Europe, there is an opportunity for Western Christians to establish greater connections and relationships with their Chinese brothers and sisters. They provide a vital connection to the amazing work of revival that has been taking place in Mainland China, allowing it to flow out from China to bless Europe and the nations. This is also another "gateway" that God is establishing for the Chinese Church to reach outwards.

Several church leaders who were called by God during Pastor Lee's first ministry tour in Europe are now operating in Beijing, Shandong, and Shanghai. When he went to visit one of them in Beijing called Brother Bu, Pastor Lee was introduced to an old man by the name of Peter Chen. Peter had been a co-worker of Brother Yun during the revival in Henan province in the 1980s. He had opened his home to use as a Bible college and were seeing many young people trained and released into ministry. On one occasion when Brother Yun had a miraculous escape from a high-security prison in Beijing, Peter and his wife had been interceding for him at home. God revealed to them that Yun had escaped from prison and so they prepared to do what they could to help him. Shortly afterwards, he appeared on their doorstep and Peter's wife was able to take him to the safe house they had prepared for his protection. Peter's daughter is now helping to run a ministry set up by Brother Yun three years ago to provide for the retired missionaries who went through the most severe persecution in the 1980s.

Kingdom Partnership

One of the reasons so many different Chinese House Church leaders were willing to contribute to the writing of this book is that they all have a strong desire to see genuine partnerships develop with the International Church. The mindset that says *the Chinese send the workers and the West sends the money* is not right. There must be a mutual honouring of the distinctiveness and the calling which God has placed on different nations of people. It is supposed to be a two-way relationship. Ephesians 4:16 says that from Christ the whole body is able to *build itself up in love, as each part does its work*. What is supplied by one part of the body is different and distinct from another part, but all are necessary. We perhaps are used to understanding this on the level of a local church congregation, but our vision has to grow larger. God is looking for a spiritual oneness that is able to transcend nations, church streams, and differences in theological interpretation. God has opened the gates to spread China out across the nations, and there is a prophetic call going out for us to begin to recognize how all this fits together with the big picture of what God is doing.

6

Power in the City

The gospel must come alive! A religiousified gospel is no gospel at all!

Pastor Rong, Shanghai

Pastor Rong is one of the increasing number of Urban House Church leaders who have had the opportunity to receive formal theological training from foreign missionaries. In 1997 he set up Aixin Church in Shanghai with no more than twenty people. Nearly sixteen years later, the church has now planted over ten congregations in and around Shanghai as well as in other cities and provinces. They have nine full-time senior pastors, ten full-time church ministers, and over a hundred lay workers. He was not entirely sure exactly how many people would consider themselves members of his church, but the number is somewhere in the thousands. According to Pastor Rong, healings and miracles have been a key component of such dramatic growth. Initially, it was simply through reading the Bible that he learned believers have the authority to heal the sick and cast out demons in the name of Jesus, so without any particularly sophisticated theology of healing other than simple faith in the name of Jesus, he began practising.

As Pastor Lee spent some time with Rong, it was clear that even in Chinese terms he carries an unusual anointing for supernatural ministry. The church carries such a reputation for healing ministry that people come from all over China to receive prayer. A man came to see him who was in a lot of pain from an unknown medical condition. After laying hands on him, Pastor Rong had a word of knowledge that the man was suffering from a particular disease of the kidneys. Rather than pray for the man to be healed on the spot, he instead told him to go and see the doctor and ask them to screen him for that particular kidney condition. To the amazement of the consultant, he was indeed suffering from that very condition and once he had received medical verification that the word of knowledge was accurate, the team at the church prayed for him and he was completely healed. When we asked him about the unique way he operates in words of knowledge, he simply said that it is all a matter of staying in tune with the Holy Spirit. He utilizes the knowledge he has of having studied dissection and anatomy before he was a pastor as a canvas on which the Holy Spirit brings revelation. He always takes time to ask God how and what he should pray for the person before they proceed. Dependency on God in prayer and a reliance on direct revelation from the Holy Spirit is a common feature among Chinese Church leaders.

In another city in Zhejiang province there lives a retired couple who had in their careers been very high-ranking government officials. Desperate to seek a cure for their daughter who was suffering from Tourette's syndrome, the anxious parents decided to contact the church after hearing of the stories of miraculous healings taking place in Shanghai. Pastor Rong invited her to come and stay at the church's healing centre. Guests are able to stay for up to two weeks with everything provided for free, the one exception being that they won't be provided with any medicine except prayer. After spending a fortnight at the healing centre, the woman was completely cured of Tourette's. The entire family gave their lives to Christ as a result and decided to open their home as a meeting place for a new church plant.

During Pastor Lee's most recent trip to Shanghai, he was able to participate directly in the ministry at the healing centre and witness its effectiveness at first hand. People who come to the centre are treated with a love and acceptance that is immediately disarming. The compassion of Christ is tangible as the team takes time to minister to the people and make them feel welcome. The wife of a mayor from another city (who wished to remain anonymous) had come to the church suffering from an incurable skin disease. The skin all over her body was dry and cracked, and she was clearly in a great deal of pain and discomfort. After she had received prayer, the skin condition completely cleared up over the following few days and she has now been able to return to work. These kinds of miracles create a ripple effect that brings an encounter with God's grace to more than just the immediate family and friends. As more and more people in positions of influence are exposed to the goodness of God, the salt and light of the presence of God in the Church is able to do its work in society.

Urban Evangelism

What causes the ministry of churches such as this to stand out in the Chinese setting is that they have managed to translate the purity of faith seen in the early days of the Rural House Church into an industrialized, urban setting. Within this context, the Urban House Church has adopted the language of "kingdom" to express their mission on earth. As Pastor Rong put it himself, their philosophy is expressing *love in real-life terms*. The gospel must have flesh on the bones, in practical application and a demonstration of power. Such an approach involves ministry to the whole person, including healing, counselling, discipleship, and equipping them to witness to their friends, family, and colleagues. The expectation is that the gospel will both multiply and adapt to the different cultural, social, and work environments in which citizens of the twenty-first century find themselves. In order to transform a nation, Christian testimony has to be found in every sphere of influence and on every level of society, not quietly hidden away in a ghettoized, exclusive community.

Of the major spheres of influence in society, one of the most strategically important is that of education. For a number of years it has been something of a running joke in Chinese popular culture that if you meet a female university student, she is quite likely to be a Christian. While this is a clear exaggeration and the humour may be somewhat lost in translation, it seems to be a big hit among Beijing taxi drivers!

A young man who was a student of Jiaotong University, one of the major academic institutions in the country, came to Aixin Church suffering from an exceptionally rare autoimmune disorder. His case was known both to the academic staff at the university and to the medical profession who were seeking to treat and study his condition. When he was 100 per cent cured after receiving prayer at the healing centre, the hospital was so astounded that they contacted the Shanghai Television Network, a state-owned television channel, to come and interview the young man concerning what had happened. As a result of the broadcast of his testimony, several university lecturers decided to visit the church to find out for themselves if there was any truth to the claim that Jesus still heals the sick today. The last we heard, several of them have already become Christian believers and others are still investigating the faith while already regularly participating in the life of the congregation. Stories such as this showcase how the preaching of the gospel with signs following is no longer relegated to the backwater, hidden places of rural China, but is on public display for the world to see. As Jesus said, *what you have heard whispered in secret, shout from the rooftops.*

We have made the point that much of what has been reported from the Chinese revival seems so far removed from the average Western Christian experience as to be almost mythical in the hearts of many believers. The reality, however, is that the modern environment facing the Urban House Church would be remarkably familiar to a Western observer. The same challenges of how to maintain a quietness of soul and a deep, intimate relationship with Christ when the world around you is getting louder, faster, and shallower are just as evident in the life of a young university graduate trying to earn a living in downtown Shanghai as they are in London or New York. Miracles and healings are a catalyst that draws people's attention to a miracle-working God, but discipleship can only take place when those encounters with God's power are allowed to translate into a lifestyle that shapes the direction of the Christian community. New believers are encouraged straight away to share the gospel with their friends and family members. In this regard, Aixin Church is quite systematic in their approach to evangelism.

One feature of the modern Chinese urban landscape is that many people live in what is referred to as a *xiaoqu* or "little community". These are typically complexes consisting of a dozen or more large apartment blocks, with an open communal garden, gym, supermarket, restaurants, or bars. These communities serve as virtually self-contained units within the residential zones of the city, as if the city itself were made up of a myriad miniature towns all jumbled together. Believers who live in the same community are encouraged to work together in evangelizing their neighbours. Personal testimony is widely regarded as one of the best ways to communicate the gospel with others. With a minimal amount of training and armed with gospel tracts and Christian literature, it is not unusual to find Christians sharing their faith with friends or colleagues on park benches or coffee shops. The communal environment of the *xiaoqu* provides a great opportunity for people to preach the gospel and pray for the sick.

In addition to the rhythm of personal evangelism, which is so much a part of Chinese Church DNA, the trendy retail district of Shanghai is a hubbub of spiritual activity at least three times a week. Evangelistic teams of up to several dozen believers will come and sing Christian worship songs through a PA system, while others hand out tracts and offer to share their testimony with passers-by. When we asked Pastor Rong about the kind of response they see, he replied that the vast majority of people are very grateful to receive the gospel tracts and listen to the singing. What seems to attract the most heartfelt response, however, is the authentic, real-life testimony of their fellow Chinese who have laid down everything to follow Jesus. A conversation will usually involve an invitation to receive prayer for healing, and without having exact figures, the church reckons that they have seen over 1,000 people healed of everything from cancer to schizophrenia. If the illness they are praying for is relatively minor, they usually pray for healing right there on the street, but if it is of a more serious nature, they will invite people to come and receive more focused ministry back at the church where they have the healing retreat centre.

It may come as a surprise that such overt evangelistic activity regularly takes place in a country that has a reputation for being hostile to Christianity. Although they have had some police resistance, the worst that has ever happened is that they have been made to stop for the day and go home, and on more than one occasion the police have simply given up and left them alone. The church's answer when challenged by the authorities is that all kinds of groups are allowed to go and advertise their products and events with live music and flyers, so why shouldn't they?

Spiritual Warfare

When East Asian believers come to the West, and especially to Western Europe, they are often quite surprised to find how little belief there is in the existence of a personal devil among their fellow Christians. People in nations where idol worship and occult practice are commonplace are much more accepting of the reality of the spiritual realm, even among the wealthy and educated. The Cultural Revolution wiped out much of the folk religion in Mainland China, which was a convoluted polytheistic hybrid of Buddhism, Daoism, and Neo-Confucianism. Historically, these religious systems became so intermixed that a single temple might have an idol that was simultaneously venerated as a Buddha, Daoist Immortal, or Neo-Confucian deity depending on which patron you asked on any given day. Most of the temples were destroyed by the Red Guards in the Cultural Revolution of the 1960s, which was also an era of intense persecution for the Church, but over the last fifteen years there has been something of a revival of interest in the world of spirits, charms, and omens. The practice of making offerings in idol temples has always persisted in territories such as Hong Kong or Taiwan, as well as ethnically Chinese regions such as Singapore or parts of Malaysia, but Mainland China was almost completely devoid of such activities for the several decades following the Cultural Revolution. In part, it would appear that the spiritual vacuum left by the eradication of traditional Chinese religion contributed even further to the spread of the gospel among Mainland Chinese.

Nowadays, it is not uncommon for wealthy businesspeople to donate millions of US dollars' worth of Chinese yuan in order to secure good luck or good health from the local temple god. When a person makes such a donation, their name is often inscribed on the wall of the temple or written on a piece of paper and kept inside. Sometimes personal items, fingernails, or strands of hair are kept in jars by the temple priests as a way of exercising control over the worshipper by inciting fear of spiritual reprisals in case they break their vows of loyalty to the temple god. This kind of activity has been on the increase again in Mainland China.

When a person who has been involved in idol worship receives the gospel, some form of deliverance from evil spirits often takes place. For many recent converts, the inscription of their name on the temple wall or the presence of their personal items in the temple is a source of fear and spiritual intimidation. Teams from Aixin Church will routinely go on expeditions to the temples to pray over any records of the new believers' past involvement with idol worship. If an inscription has been made, they will either paint over it or scratch it out, and any personal items will be removed and destroyed. They have a number of testimonies of new converts who have been set free from demonic spirits as a result of this unusual ministry!

The church will send these teams to bless the home of anyone who is worried that they might have a problem with evil spirits or curses placed over them, which is itself a great opportunity to share the gospel. Pastor Rong related how at one point there was a reality television programme in Shanghai where they had set up video cameras to try to catch evidence of paranormal activity in two buildings that were said to be haunted. He decided that this was a good excuse to go and pray over the building and cast out any evil spirits that might be causing a problem. I'm not sure if the television show ever did find any evidence of paranormal activity after his visit...

Of the stories of spiritual warfare and deliverance, one of the most dramatic took place in early January 2013. Pastor Rong had been contacted by a group of people from the Lagu tribe – a non-Chinese people group in Yunnan province. Yunnan is a southern region with a tropical climate and home to many ethno-linguistic groups whose languages and cultures are completely distinct from the Chinese. Some of these tribes have received a good deal of missionary input, whereas others are almost completely unreached by the gospel. Part of the missionary mandate to the Chinese Church is to help bring the gospel to these unreached tribes.

The Lagu tribe had lived in acute fear of a several-hundred-year-old totem pole that stood on their ancestral land. According to the tribe, anyone who attempted to move the pole either fell seriously ill or else was struck dead on the spot. Even during the Cultural Revolution, the tribe said that ten red guards had died instantly while trying to destroy the relic. As a result, no one else had dared to go anywhere near it, even though many of the tribespeople had already become Christians and renounced idol worship. Pastor Rong told us that, when he arrived on the scene, he sensed there was a demonic power attached to the totem pole. After prayer, he told the people to keep out of the way while he proceeded to overturn the totem pole and throw it into the nearby river. At that very moment, his young grandson suddenly fell seriously ill back in Shanghai and was rushed into hospital, although after prayer he recovered and was able to return home. This story carries echoes of the eighth-century account of Saint Boniface who dared to cut down the sacred oak tree of the Germanic pagans in what is often considered to be the moment that marked the Christianization of the Germanic peoples.

A Powerful God and a Defeated Devil

To the Chinese Church, there is no question as to who is in charge. A striking theme that recurs throughout all the interviews and testimonies with church leaders from across the whole country is that they really believe God is in control. It reminds me of Jesus' words to Pilate in John 19:11: *You would have no power over me unless it had been given to you from above.* In other words, the Church believes that any season of persecution that has come against them has been allowed by God in order to see a greater manifestation of His glory come through their nation. This does not mean that the Church is passive in the face of such persecution, and in several areas the Church is presenting an open and powerful challenge to the ungodly laws that are being used as justification for the harassment of Christians. It does mean that you are unlikely to hear a Chinese Church pastor complain or lament the lack of religious freedoms that they have experienced in their nation. They believe that Jesus is on the throne and they are working for Him. Instead, they are far more likely to seek God for revelation as to how to respond to such persecution, trusting that God is working behind the scenes to bring about greater redemption to the Chinese people and beyond.

There are two general spheres where we see the confrontation between the powers of light and the powers of darkness most clearly, and in both of them the Chinese Church recognizes that God is huge and the devil is tiny. The first is in the sociopolitical sphere, where there is an ongoing contention among people in places of influence in society or governments to give room either to righteousness or unrighteousness in the nation. The second is where there is a more immediate confrontation with demonic spirits that are oppressing people who have been involved in occult practice and need to be set free. The Western Church often does not understand the spiritual authority that has been given to us by Christ. Being church leaders ourselves in the United Kingdom, we have noticed that believers can display a real lack of confidence in dealing with the overt opposition of spiritual powers through prayer and the power of the name of Jesus. Meanwhile in the political sphere, the Western Church is often either disengaged altogether or suffers from being overly politicized and reduced to a "special interest group" within society. It tends to be that the British Church is more disengaged, while the American Church is overly politicized. In both countries, fear abounds about the perceived loss of Christian freedoms. People are afraid of the devil! The Chinese Church has learned to face off against the powers of darkness without fear, and that gives them a strength and a confidence to continue fighting for the kingdom of God to be revealed in their nation whether times are good or times are hard.

I would like to close this chapter with another two stories of how the supernatural power of Jesus to set people free is greater than the power of the devil to keep them in chains. These stories both come from Pastor Lee's wife concerning her early Christian life in Malaysia. When we were first getting to know each other, she asked me how open I was to believing stories of the supernatural. In their experience, British Christians were quite sceptical of the spiritual nature of the world, which many growing up in an East Asian culture take for granted.

During the Cultural Revolution, her great-aunt was tortured and killed for refusing to deny her faith in Christ. Her great-uncle was then told that his whole family would be killed if he did not give up his faith. Under such intense pressure, he agreed to renounce his Christian faith and never speak of it again. From that time on, none of her family had been Christian believers. It was a great shock to them when she became Christian as a young teenager. She had been brought up in a traditional Chinese environment, where the family regularly participated in ancestor worship and various occult practices. Her Christianity was unacceptable in such a family and she was even physically beaten on a number of occasions because of her faith.

One day she went to the house of her relative who was a very famous spirit medium in Malaysia. People would come from all over the country to receive magic spells and charms from him, and he had a reputation for being a person of great supernatural power. On this particular day, he was in his study writing magic spells, when something interrupted him. He started to shout out, *who are these Christians who have come into my house? Please leave at once because I am unable to contact the spirit who speaks to me as long as you are in here!* The light that she carried as a disciple of Christ dispelled the darkness! The entire family have since come back to Christ.

The second story concerned the testimony of a Sunday school teacher from their church. When she was a girl, her family had the habit of playing a traditional Chinese divination game where two people would hold up a wicker basket with a pair of chopsticks. A brush would be tied to the base of the wicker basket and left to hang freely from the string. The participants would then ask questions to a spirit, and the brush would begin to write on a piece of paper in response. After she became a Christian, she was no longer willing to carry on this occult game, although the rest of the family would regularly try to encourage her to come and *play with the spirit*. On one day, she had been praying for her family while they were in the other room trying to contact the spirit with the chopsticks and the brush. To their bemusement nothing was happening, so they asked the spirit why it wouldn't speak to them anymore. Then the brush began to move and wrote the four Chinese characters *Ye Su Ji Du*, which translates as "Jesus Christ". They asked the spirit what that meant, and the brush moved again, writing, *The true God is rebuking me*. After that they were no longer able to get any response from the brush. As a result, the entire family gave their lives to Christ, and the framed piece of paper is still hanging on their wall today as a testimony of the goodness of God!

The Western Pilgrimage

A mountain cannot block the way of the road, it will make its own way through.

Chinese proverb – from **Journey to the West**

An Ancient Dream

In China's history, the West has often symbolized a gateway to another world of spiritual pilgrimage. It is a folk saying in China that when a person dies, their spirit makes *the western crossing*. It was from the west that Buddhism entered China from India, influencing the culture of many subsequent generations, and it was through the traders along the western Silk Road that the ancient Chinese heard stories of far-off empires and mysterious lands. There is even a possibility that the main protagonist of the Tibetan literary classic *Gesar*, who came from a place called "Trom", was actually based on stories about Caesar of Rome. For the Chinese Church, the sense of spiritual affinity with the lands west of the Himalayan Mountains is the seed of a God-given destiny, which concerns God's heart and calling for the Chinese people. There is a spiritual and cultural inheritance unique to every tribe and nation in the world. This inheritance becomes distorted, degraded, or misaligned apart from Christ's redemption, but as God brings His kingdom into the nations, we should expect to see the recovery and fulfilment of that inheritance. For many Chinese leaders, the sense of being drawn towards the West that has existed for thousands of years was part of God's plan to call them and bring them home – not to Buddhist India, but to Jerusalem.

That sense of pilgrimage is described in Psalm 84:4 *Blessed are those whose strength is in you, in whose hearts are the highways of Zion* or ... *whose hearts are set on pilgrimage.* (ESV) Whereas the Catholic view of pilgrimage places great emphasis on the destination, the ancient Celtic Church which derives its roots from the desert fathers of Asia Minor understood the journey itself to be equally or even more important. Three aspects make up this kind of pilgrimage: the outward, physical journey in response to the calling; the inward, spiritual journey into deeper relationship with Christ; and the journey of mission, which spreads the life of the kingdom to all along the way.

The Back to Jerusalem Vision

Almost a century ago, a move of God broke out in several different places across China apparently without direct connection to each another. The relatively small number of believers scattered around the country, some connected with Western missionaries, began to sense a prophetic calling towards Jerusalem. This would mark the point when the fledgling Chinese Church first began to embrace the idea of cross-cultural missions. By the 1940s, it had become a trend in many Bible colleges and training centres to encourage young people to form small evangelistic bands, which would be sent towards China's frontier regions. The vision was to reach the tribes and ethnic minorities concentrated on China's western borders with the gospel, as well as the Chinese people living in the villages they passed through.

In one such Bible college, the story goes that a young lady who was a student suddenly felt impressed by the Holy Spirit one day that they as a group needed to go to Jerusalem. Being illiterate and without a strong knowledge of the Scriptures, she wasn't sure if Jerusalem even existed at all, or if it had existed at one time, whether or not it was still there. Because of this, she really wasn't confident that it was God speaking to her, but when she finally plucked up the courage to share the message with the other members of the college, she found that several other people in the meeting had all received identical or similar words. Theirs was a pure and simple faith and, having heard what they understood to be God's call on their lives, they began to send people on foot to the north-west border region of China with only the most basic of supplies.

Two groups in particular played key roles in this movement. The first is called the Northwest Spiritual

Movement, which appears to have been centred around a Bible college called the *Ledao Yuan* in Shandong province. This college had previously been associated with American missionaries, and during the Sino-Japanese war it was taken over and used as a concentration camp by the occupying Japanese forces. The second was led by Pastor Mark Ma, and is known in English as the Back to Jerusalem Evangelistic Band. It was launched from the Northwest Bible Institute in Shaanxi province, founded by Hudson Taylor's grandson, James Hudson Taylor II. The missionaries sent out from these two colleges gradually made their way to Xinjiang province, which used to be called Eastern Turkestan. It is a large, desert region of China populated primarily by the Uyghur people, the largest Islamic group in China. Xinjiang was the entry point of the Silk Road into Chinese territory, and represents the main access point into the Middle East. When the Communist Party took over China, they closed the borders and this first wave of missionaries was unable to continue past Xinjiang. Many of them were martyred or died in prison, having been branded enemies of the state by the new regime, but some of those who survived have stayed in Xinjiang ever since and are still alive today, watching and praying for China, the Middle East, and for Jerusalem. When Pastor Lee and the team met with one of these old missionaries, the first thing he said to them was, *Young people! Are you on your way to Jerusalem?* He then proceeded to stand and sing through the theme songs of the Northwest Spiritual Movement, which he could still remember after all those years.

Mrs He Enzheng is one of the members of the Back to Jerusalem Evangelistic Band who is still in Xinjiang today. Now ninety-seven years old, she has firmly refused to go back, saying that she would remain faithful to the vision she had received from heaven. She and her husband were newly married when they arrived in the area, but shortly afterwards he tragically died in prison after being arrested and branded an enemy of the state. For over sixty years she has knelt down to pray every single morning for China, Jerusalem, and the vision to send missionaries out of China into the Middle East. She has become something of a legendary figure among the Chinese House Churches. Those who want to visit have to pass through three levels of House Church security because she is under such close surveillance from the Public Security Bureau (PSB).

When Pastor Lee and his wife were on their way to see He Enzheng with several other foreigners, the restaurant they were in was suddenly surrounded by PSB agents. The Christian workers in Xinjiang are prepared for anything, and they had a contingency escape plan in place for just such a situation. Pastor Lee was able to sneak out of the restaurant with the foreigners and pass them through several different cars and escorts in order to lose track of the agents before finally getting them to the house where He Enzheng was staying. When Pastor Lee walked towards the apartment block, he made eye contact with a man who was standing by the side of the road. Although they hadn't ever seen each other before, the man was able to tell that this was the visitor he had been told to expect. Without saying a word, he turned around and began to walk. Pastor Lee followed, until a subtle motion from this bodyguard indicated to him that they had arrived at the right place, then the man just continued to walk on by as if he had nothing to do with them.

He Enzheng will only accept visitors if she has heard directly from God that He has sent them, otherwise they will be turned away by her bodyguards. For many years she has discipled young believers in Xinjiang and missionaries who have come from within central China to serve there, but there is always the risk that people might be put in danger by a lapse in security. When Pastor Lee went in to see her, she suddenly exclaimed, *Oh it's time for the gospel to go forward! What God has promised He will accomplish!* Even after all these years, her mind is incredibly sharp and her memory of the vision is crystal clear: the Chinese Church has been called by God to take the gospel back to Jerusalem. She spoke of how in the 1940s those early pioneers made their way on foot up towards Xinjiang. They didn't carry any provisions with them, but simply trusted that God would provide their needs along the way. On one occasion she was hungry and had asked God to give her some food. All of a sudden she came across a loaf of bread that had been left at the side of the road. Giving thanks to God, she and her friends shared the bread and continued on into the local village to preach the gospel. The following day she discovered that the bread had actually been poisoned by the locals as a trap to kill wild dogs! The missionaries had eaten it and miraculously suffered no ill effects.

When the church leaders learned of her life's vision to go to Jerusalem, they offered to buy her a plane ticket to Israel. She adamantly refused, saying that since God had told them to walk, she wouldn't go anywhere unless it was on foot. Pastor Lee had come up with a plan. On the trip they had brought a messianic rabbi along with them from Israel to meet with her. The rabbi had carried a stone from Jerusalem along with him, and to honour the sacrifice and faithfulness of Mrs He and the other missionaries, she was able to set foot on a piece of Jerusalem while they prayed together for her and the vision. The rabbi was moved to tears as he saw how much the Chinese believers loved the Jews and fervently prayed for them, and for peace to be on Jerusalem as well as the whole of the Middle East.

Understanding the Vision

A good deal has already been said about the Back to Jerusalem vision as it exists today. For a while, it was unclear to many Western observers just to what degree the vision had been adopted by the Chinese Church at large, but it is now evident that the vision for a missionary China has become almost universal among the House Church networks. In the most general of terms, the Chinese Church understands the Back to Jerusalem vision in the following way: the gospel originally went out from Jerusalem. From there, it spread out both east and west until the rise of Islam for the most part closed things down in Asia, while the west continued to be open. Rome was the centre of world evangelization until the dawn of the Evangelical/Protestant missions movements, at which point God raised up the British Empire to be the primary vehicle for the spread of the gospel out to all nations. From there, the burden of first responsibility shifted across the Atlantic to the United States in the twentieth century, and then South Korea began to rise as a leader in world missions. From South Korea, the mandate and anointing for the next step is now passing to China, which God has specifically prepared in the next season to lead the way into the Middle East, an area dominated by Islam, which has become increasingly closed to Western input. Everything then is able to come full circle as the gospel of the kingdom is brought to all the unreached nations between China and Israel, before finally coming "back to Jerusalem". The modern Chinese Church sees its 65-year history of growth and development under persecution – isolated from foreign intervention – as a part of the unique training ground in which God has placed them so that they will be equipped to engage with the Muslim world. What appeared to be a great obstacle to the gospel going out from China has actually become the means for China's preparation.

This vision may seem very simplistic, but we must remember that we all know in part and prophesy in part, and this is just one element of a much larger picture. It is a broad mandate that was conceived in a simple and pure form in the hearts of those early pioneers, and it has now filtered through into the wider body of Christ in China, pointing them towards their destiny as a missionary nation. But now the present challenge facing the Chinese Church is how this vision grows up into spiritual maturity along with the rest of what God is doing and saying, not only in China but in the Church worldwide.

The simple revivalist approach of the Rural House Church has not been particularly effective when applied in the foreign environment. A number of churches have already tried to send missionaries out into various Middle Eastern regions, but the majority have had to return, discovering that they were in fact ill equipped to operate cross-culturally. We know of one woman who spent eight months in Xinjiang as a cross-cultural missionary, after which she relocated to Beijing to join the seminary at Zion Church, having found that the level of equipping and support she had received was not sufficient to make an impact in the area.

There are some areas where Chinese missionaries are already being very effective, most notably North Korea where their identity as Chinese citizens affords unique access into what is arguably the most closed nation on the planet today. Meanwhile the vast majority of House Church leaders are saying that they believe it will be another fifteen to twenty years before they are ready to send people internationally on any real scale. One thing is for certain, however – this is what they are preparing for.

Raising up the Highways

I will turn all my mountains into roads, and my highways will be raised up. See they come from afar – some from the north, some from the west, and some from the land of Sinim.

(Isaiah 49:11–12)

Just as God is establishing the gates to the cities, He is also raising up the highways of mission. The Chinese Church believes that the reference to Sinim in Isaiah 49 is a specific prophecy about them. In the Chinese Bible, it is translated as *the people from Qin*, which is the name of China's first imperial dynasty ("Qin" is pronounced "Chin" and is where we get the English word "China"). In actual fact many believe that the reference to mountains becoming roads and highways being raised up is literally being fulfilled right now. In 2010 the Chinese government announced plans for the most ambitious railway project ever conceived. Three high-speed rail lines are being prepared that will link China to the West. The first will run north through Mongolia and Russia towards Moscow, the old route of the Trans-Siberian railway. The second is dubbed the New Silk Road, and is expected to run parallel to the ancient Silk Road from Urumqi in Xinjiang, passing through Kazakhstan, Uzbekistan, and Turkmenistan on the way to Berlin. The third line, which is already partly complete, runs south to Singapore via Myanmar and the Buddhist world. These projects are expected to be completed by 2025, and have involved negotiations with seventeen different countries. As of 2012, an agreement has been reached between China and Turkey to extend the planned third line from Pakistan, Iran, and Iraq through Turkey and into Europe, after which it will eventually link to London and Madrid.

What we are seeing is a rapidly changing global landscape, where China establishes itself as the key cultural and economic partner of the Middle East. Just as the imperial ambitions of Great Britain in the eighteenth and nineteenth centuries allowed the gospel to travel via trade routes across the globe, so these new highways open up limitless possibilities to bring the Chinese Church closer to their dream of sharing the love of God in these unreached nations. There is a strong prophetic sense within the Chinese Church that Xinjiang is the key to everything. On one occasion, Pastor Lee was praying and asking God why He was raising up China as a missionary nation. The Holy Spirit told him to look up at the map of China on the wall of his office and to look specifically at the north-west region – Xinjiang. He sensed God say that Xinjiang would be a preparation ground to train the Chinese in how to engage with the Islamic world. God has given the Chinese an opportunity to learn what it is to integrate and become one with the people, being immersed in the culture and understanding their different way of life. Xinjiang is the place where eyes are opened and vision is expanded. The Han Chinese who have moved into the area have struggled to overcome the culture shock and ethnic prejudices that confront them. With God's grace, however, many are testifying that the love they have for the indigenous people, and for the Middle Eastern and Turkic nations, is deepening and growing more real with each passing day.

The New Pioneers

While in Israel in 2005, Pastor Lee met a young House Church leader who was friends with a Communist Party official and his wife. Many years before, they had lived in a house neighbouring the place where Brother Yun and some of his friends were in hiding from the authorities. For days this official was convinced that there were illegal missionaries hiding next door, but despite his efforts he could find no evidence that they were there. He had hoped that he would give himself a good chance for a promotion if he were able to help the government track down these wanted criminals! Every day he would look down from his roof into the open courtyard of the neighbouring house, but there was no sign of anyone there. In reality, Brother Yun and the others were praying and worshipping aloud in the courtyard, but somehow this official had been supernaturally blinded to their presence. A while later he became a Christian and came to learn that Brother Yun had indeed been hiding next door to him those years before, but God had not allowed him to see it! They are now active supporters of the Back to Jerusalem vision.

Mr and Mrs Huang (not their real name) are a young couple belonging to the new generation of pioneers who have responded to God's call to the borderlands. They originally come from Shenzhen, one of the cities designated as a special economic zone on China's south coast. Shenzhen is one of the fastest growing cities in the country, and is the southern centre for financial services and many high-tech multinationals. In addition to being one of China's main shipping ports, it is also widely considered to be among the most spiritually open cities to the gospel. Since 2010, the Chinese government has also granted the city of Kashgar in Xinjiang special economic status, and Shenzhen has been drafted in as a patron city, contributing a percentage of its total revenue for Kashgar to be developed. The Huangs believe that there is an important prophetic significance to the linking of these two cities. Shenzhen is one of the most open areas, while Xinjiang is the most closed along with Tibet, being predominantly Islamic. Having seen a film on the Back to Jerusalem vision distributed among the Chinese House Churches, they were inspired by the story of the early pioneer missionaries of the Northwest Spiritual Movement and the Back to Jerusalem Evangelistic Band and decided to take a trip to see the area for themselves.

Xinjiang is still one of the least polluted regions of China, with beautiful blue skies and unspoilt landscapes. As their plane touched down, something in their hearts felt as if they had come home. A great sandstorm rose up out of nowhere, and they felt that God was trying to give them a sign concerning the significance of the area and the spiritual activity overhead. They prayed together with a migrant missionary who had been in Kashgar for five years, specifically asking God about the Chinese government's plans for economic investment into the province. As they were praying, they sensed God lead them to Proverbs 21:1, *The heart of the king is in the hand of the Lord, and he directs it like a channel of water wherever he wills.* To them this was confirmation that the government's economic programme was part of God's strategy for the area, and they felt that He was looking for people who would be willing to stay there long term. In response to this calling, they immediately purchased a house and moved to the region in September 2010 to start an agricultural business. They say that their purpose is not to evangelize or try to plant churches, but just to pour out the love of God onto the city and its people, and plough the ground in prayers for others to follow. Every day they intercede for the whole region, sometimes praying in –20°C temperatures while kneeling on the floor. They have found that many pastors and businesspeople have tried to set things up in Xinjiang, but it seems that only those who are willing to base themselves long term in the region are able to see success. Through prayer, their sense from the Holy Spirit is that there are many others in different spheres such as education or business who God is preparing to come to Xinjiang, and especially Kashgar, to establish a foundation for the Back to Jerusalem vision.

It appears that God is using commerce to prepare the way for the gospel in Xinjiang. Because of the government's investment programme, they have been encouraging many Han Chinese businesses to move into the region. Unfortunately this has not been particularly well received by the local Uyghur population, who increasingly view the Chinese as an occupying force trying to dilute the culture and exploit the resources of the region. The strong tensions running under the surface erupted into violent clashes in July 2009 when riots in the capital of Urumqi saw several hundred Chinese killed and many injured while Chinese businesses were attacked and vandalized.

One day while Mrs Huang was praying in a field, she felt the Holy Spirit say to her,

> *My child, you have come to true understanding of my will and my heart. Now I want you to understand what my will is for this region, and to draw others into that same revelation of my love for these people. Pay the price for the next generation of people to come through.*

She felt that the riots had brought about a purging of those who had come to the area simply to pursue financial gain. Before the uprising, many investors were looking for ways to establish businesses in the Uyghur territory, but afterwards some 60,000 Han Chinese decided to leave. Now very few people are willing to take the risk, and a significant proportion of the remaining businesspeople investing in the area are Christians who have come with a genuine heart for the area.

Springs of Reconciliation

At Christmas 2012, the government issued a strict warning to the Christians in Xinjiang not to carry out any open celebrations. They are so afraid of the ethnic tensions in the area that any open Christian work in the area is met with severe consequences. Despite this fact, there is one Christian group who were allowed to have a Christmas celebration: the believers from the east coast city of Wenzhou. The government recognizes that the economic investment provided by the Wenzhou businesses is so vital to the future of their plans in the area, and as a result they seem to have been granted special consideration. It just so happens that a large proportion of Wenzhou businesspeople in Xinjiang are Christians who have a heart for the Back to Jerusalem vision! This is one example of how the social and economic influence of the Chinese Church is beginning to increase its influence and freedom to act.

On 6 July 2010, a team of intercessors from the Chinese Church went to the desert of Aksu, 500 km from Kashgar. Their prayer was that God would release His love to dissolve the hatred between the Han Chinese and the Uyghurs, and also to ask for God's forgiveness for the sin of the shedding of innocent blood in the riots. While they were praying, water started to bubble up from hundreds of little openings in the ground. Before long, water was gushing out everywhere, transforming the whole desert area around them into a huge lake of water! When we asked them about it, they sent us photographs (see photo section) along with a video showing the water springing up out of the ground. Isaiah 43:19 says, *See, I am doing a new thing! Now it springs up; do you not perceive it? I am making a way in the wilderness and streams in the wasteland.* God is doing a new thing in the region of Xinjiang that is both miraculous and sovereign. It is a sign to the Chinese Church that the next phase of world revival is at hand!

From Xi'an to Zion

The thing that China needs more than anything else is spiritual fathers. We have to learn to be sons before we can understand what it means to be fathers ourselves, otherwise we will never be effective in bringing hope to the Middle East – to the world's biggest orphan, Ishmael.

Brother Gao Quanfu, Xi'an to Zion Initiative

The Homecoming Conference

In 2006 in Shenzhen, a small group of Urban and Rural House Church leaders set out with a vision to create a forum for Chinese and overseas church leaders to be able to connect and relate together. Over the first two years they organized seven gatherings, with increasing numbers of leaders attending each time. Representatives from Macau, Hong Kong, Taiwan, and beyond started attending, each time gathering without a set agenda or prearranged conference speakers. They would simply worship together informally, pray for one another, share what they felt God was saying, and work for reconciliation and unity across the many different groups represented. To begin with, the whole format seemed totally crazy to the Chinese mindset. Some just couldn't grasp the point of travelling at their own expense and risking trouble with the authorities just for what they saw as an extended worship meeting: *We have been worshipping the Lord all year – why on earth would we want to sit around and do nothing for days with leaders from outside China who don't even teach?* This encapsulates the feelings of many of the Chinese Church leaders in the beginning. Some decided to stop attending, but overall the conference gathered so much momentum that by 2010 they had to relocate to Hong Kong in order to avoid serious problems with the government.

Since the 1950s, the Chinese Church has been left alone. The reconnection with the overseas Chinese territories and the Western Church has provided an opportunity for the re-establishing of spiritual father–son relationships between them. For many years the House Churches suffered from a kind of spiritual warlordism or "empire building". Although the historical denominationalism was absent, the young leaders set up their own territories and systems of church, without necessarily any connection or honouring towards their counterparts in other areas. Sometimes the Rural House Church networks especially have been very hierarchical in their structure, where people defer loyally but at times blindly to the next level of leadership above them. Behind this is an echo of traditional Chinese family values of respect for elders, but it can at times be in danger of cultivating a system that is more controlling than it is releasing towards people. It is also incredibly lonely and isolated at the top of these vast organizations. One Chinese friend of mine joked that even the terminology used in some of the networks to refer to elders and leaders in the Church sounded just like the words used by the Triads – Chinese organized crime families!

The need to control and create factions away from others arises from fear. The Bible teaches us that fear only exists where the perfect love of God does not (1 John 4:18), and it is a manifestation of the orphanhood that comes from living life apart from the love of Father God. The Chinese Church has had to grow in isolation, away from the spiritual fathers who could impart a revelation of their true identity and serve as a physical representation of the Father's love. Orphans learn that they have to fight for everything, and that they can trust no one. There is no sense of security in the heart of an orphan because they have grown up without the security of home. Under the desert wilderness of persecution and isolation, the Chinese Church has had to fight to discover its own identity and to survive in a hostile environment. Many Chinese leaders still carry that sense of orphanhood within them. Where this is the case, a person's spiritual life may be characterized by great exploits of faith, but they will arise from a works-based mentality of slavery rather than the joy and rest of true adoption. Without that deep, heartfelt revelation of the acceptance and rest in the love of Papa God in Christ, the kingdom of God, which is supposed to be based on family and relationship, becomes instead a thing of systems and religion.

The Homecoming Conference, or Homecoming Movement as it is often referred to in Chinese, is the first major step towards a form of national recognition and releasing that can come when leaders of different church streams gather together. It represents the most encouraging move towards a genuine and lasting unity in Chinese House Church history. In the past there has been an elitism surrounding church leaders, and they would very rarely come together to honour and bless one another. Now, even the senior figures of the five big church networks have joined the movement and are giving it their full support. The annual conference now sees as many as 20,000 people (including government agents!) attending, with this number expected to grow to as many as 30,000 in 2013. The conference in 2012 was particularly significant: as the representatives from the Western Church, Bill Johnson and Chuck Pierce brought a key to give to the Chinese Church as a prophetic sign that the authority to lead the way in the next season has passed from America and the West to China. At the same time, the leaders of the five church networks publicly confessed that they recognized each other as one family in Christ and were laying down their own banners of independence. Two generations of church leaders were able to stand together for the first time on the platform and declare the arrival of the kingdom of God in China, with many prayers of thanksgiving offered for the sacrifice and service of Western missionaries in their nation.

The Xi'an to Zion Initiative

Brother Gao Quanfu is a House Church leader in the old Chinese capital city of Xi'an. This was at one time the terminal stop on the ancient Silk Road, and it is one of the major cultural centres in China. In the mid 1990s, Brother Gao had a vision in which a teardrop from God's face fell down onto him. All of a sudden he was overwhelmed by a sense of love and longing for the children of Israel to come to know Jesus as their messiah. He could not stop crying and interceding for days after this experience. In response to this encounter, their church has held 24–7 prayer vigils for Israel and the nations ever since. When Chinese believers come to Christ, they usually find they have a spontaneous love for Israel and a burden to pray for the Jewish people. The first known entry of the Diaspora Jews into China was as early as the seventh century, with the most famous community being that of the Kaifeng Jews, which still exists today. The Chinese emperor welcomed the Jews into China, praising the nobility of their religion and culture. In 1938, Shanghai became a place for nearly 30,000 Jewish refugees escaping the holocaust in Europe who had nowhere else they could go. Even among secular Chinese there is a fascination with the history of Israel and the Jewish people, and it is notable that there has historically never been any anti-Semitism in the country. Israel and its spiritual significance is a subject of much controversy in the Western Church, but I think that one of the simplest yet most profound statements on the matter was made by Brother Gao:

> *Israel is a sacrificial nation. Everything the Jews have suffered over the centuries has been because they rejected the Messiah, but this had to happen so that the nations could be reconciled to God. Israel is like the eldest son among the nations, being made to wait outside for all the others to come back home first before he is able to come in himself. What should our response to Israel be? It should be one of gratitude!*

Abraham is the physical ancestor of the Jewish people, and he is called one of God's best friends. God's longing is for all of His lost children to come home, regardless of what tribe or language they come from, but the Bible points out that Israel is *loved on account of the patriarchs* (Romans 11:28). What I think this means is that when someone has a best friend, he will inevitably love his friend's children too! For us as the Church to be one with our heavenly Father means for our hearts and our affections also to be one with His. Because of this, I think that regardless of what our theology is concerning the nation of Israel, the Christian thing to do is to express our gratitude to God by praying for them and seeking for God's peace and salvation to be poured out over them; in other words, to *pray for the peace of Jerusalem.* This is not something that carries any kind of spiritual controversy in the Chinese Church, and they are all the better for it.

As well as Isaac, the father of Israel, Abraham had another son called Ishmael. In Genesis 16:13, God reveals Himself to Hagar the mother of Ishmael as "El Roi", the God who Sees. Whenever the Scripture calls God by a new name it is revealing something unique about His character that has never been seen before. The name of Jesus for instance means "God saves", because He is the revelation of God's salvation on earth. When God spoke to Hagar, He promised that He would also bless Ishmael as well as Isaac and make him into a great nation, but that there would be a wildness and a contention that would come from him towards the other nations. The Islamic peoples traditionally identify themselves as Abraham's descendants through Ishmael, as opposed to the Jewish people being descended from Isaac. Perhaps the most ancient and profound conflict between two brothers over their father's love is being played out in the Middle East today. According to the Bible, Abraham sent Ishmael away when God said that the inheritance was to be given to his younger brother Isaac instead of to him. Brother Gao calls Ishmael and the Islamic peoples "the world's biggest orphan". It is interesting to note that one of the things which people from an Islamic background find the hardest to accept about Christianity is the concept of God as a father. In order to be prepared to take the gospel into the Middle East, the Chinese Church needs to be free of that same orphan spirit which has kept the area locked down in fear and conflict for generations.

Abraham's Lost Son

On 12 November 2006, Brother Gao was praying at his usual time of 3 a.m. While he was in worship, the Holy Spirit came upon him powerfully and said, *I want you to gather a team of people who will drive from Xi'an to Zion. I have already chosen those who will take part.* He set about communicating the plan through his contact network, and, supported by the newly formed Homecoming Movement, the vision to make a prophetic journey along the Old Silk road from China to Jerusalem spread throughout the whole country. Thousands of people applied to join the team, and through much prayer and many discussions with different church leaders, they settled on a group of fifteen House Church pastors from nine different provinces to make up the expedition. Finally on 8 September 2008, the team was ready to set out on their journey through Pakistan, Iran, Turkey, Syria, Jordan, and finally Israel, supported by over a million intercessors from the Chinese-speaking world who had committed to pray for them. Before they set out, one of the team had a vision. They saw Abraham standing there with his sleeves soaked with tears. They were tears for his lost son Ishmael and all of his spiritual descendants to come home. This was a key revelation to them of God's heart for the Muslim peoples of the Middle East, and helped to guide their prayers as they went.

At first they made their way to Xinjiang province, which would be their last port of call before crossing over China's border into Pakistan. Brother Gao had a prophetic word that it was now time to *draw back the bow* in Xinjiang to get ready for the arrow to be fired. They spent a number of days ministering to the missionaries in the area and meeting with the early pioneers who were still living there. They were able to see Mrs Zhang Guquan, one of the founding members of the Northwest Spiritual Movement and receive her blessing. She was moved to tears as they asked her to pray for the anointing to be passed on to them as the next generation. Not long after the journey had been completed, God called Mrs Zhang home. Another of the early pioneers called Brother Tian also went home within a few days of praying for the team and passing on his blessing. They had finally seen the beginnings of the fulfilment of a vision carried for more than six decades. On visiting Mrs He Enzheng, who was ninety-two years old at the time and is one of the last remaining pioneers still alive today, she remarked that God had kept her alive all those years for her to see that day when the Chinese Church was finally able to cross the border. She turned her eyes towards heaven and called out the name of her husband who had been martyred nearly sixty years before, *Maijia, can you see? The Chinese Church is finally going out!*

The first stage of the trip was a time of great testing for all involved. Almost immediately the team was plagued by divisions. Most of the fifteen team members were highly capable leaders with many hundreds of people in their churches. Each of them was used to being the one in charge! God spoke to Hao Xin, one of the women on the team, that unless they could all sort out their differences, they would not be able to leave the country. They had set out in faith without having had time to prepare all of the visas necessary for the trip, and were relying on God for a miraculous intervention to get all the paperwork arranged in time. Time was of the essence because the country was about to be on holiday for the Mid-Autumn Festival. If they could not get the visas arranged before the start of the holiday, they would have to turn back. Finally at the last possible moment, there was a breakthrough in their dealings with the authorities, and they were granted permission to go. Brother Gao joked afterwards that if the visas hadn't come through they would have had to stone him for being a false prophet! The divisions between them that were exposed on the first part of the trip were a prophetic sign to the Chinese Church that a genuine spirit of unity must be present throughout before they are able to step into their destiny. One of the congregation members from Brother Gao's church in Xi'an had prepared enough bread and wine for the team to take communion every day of the trip. They said that it was taking communion that saved them from having to disband and go home. No matter what arguments had taken place during the day, every evening they would gather together to pray for one another and take communion. If anyone had anything against someone else on the team, they would have to ask for forgiveness and be reconciled in the presence of God.

Into the Middle East

As they made their way into Pakistan, the team found themselves caught in the middle of a civil war with the Taliban. Pakistan and China are close allies in the region, with a lot of Chinese investment going into the country. The Pakistani government provided the team with an armed escort to protect them while they were trying to make their way through. At one point, they felt compelled by God to stop and intercede for the nation. Several years later, when the news broke that Osama Bin Laden had been killed in Pakistan, one of the team members saw on the television that the very place God had moved them to stop and pray had been right next to the secret Al Qaeda compound where he had been hiding!

The reception they received from the Pakistani people was incredibly warm and welcoming. There is a specific law in the country that protects Chinese citizens, meaning that it is a different criminal offence to assault a Chinese person than it is to assault anyone else. One afternoon they had stopped to refuel their cars. A man wearing white robes and a turban and carrying an AK-47 assault rifle over his shoulder came up to Brother Gao with a big grin on his face. *You are Chinese*, he said in broken English. *I am Taliban. We welcome you to Pakistan!* The advent of the Islamic festival of Eid provided a ceasefire in the fighting that was just enough of a window to allow them to cross through the country. They left with a strong sense that in the future many people would be martyred for their faith in Pakistan, but that God would use their witness to bring a multitude of people to Christ across the nation.

The story was similar across the rest of the Middle Eastern nations. They carried out more intercession in Iran than anywhere else. Several of them had an unusual vision of a bird with a head that kept changing from a chicken, to a duck, to other birds. They felt the interpretation was that a particular spirit of deception was attacking the Iranian people and they interceded specifically against the effects of that deception. They also prayed for peace between Iran and Israel. When they were getting closer to the Israeli border, they realized that they might encounter a big problem entering the country on account of the visa stamps from all the nations they had just travelled through. Back in the United Kingdom, Pastor Lee was able to use his contacts in Israel to grant them special permission to enter the country. From the time they set out from Xi'an to when they crossed the border into Israel exactly forty days and forty nights had passed to the hour, although they only realized this afterwards. The sight of fifteen Chinese pilgrims having just driven across the Middle East was a novelty to say the least. A national news network wanted to interview them on live television, but being concerned about security they declined. Pastor Lee and his wife were able to make the interview on behalf of the Chinese Church. When they told the interviewer that they represented 100 million Chinese Christian believers who love Israel and are praying for peace in the region, she was moved to tears live on camera. As a result of that interview, the Israeli government changed their policy on Chinese visitors to the country, issuing tourist visas to Chinese citizens for the first time since a ban several years before.

The entire journey was edited into a twelve-episode documentary and distributed throughout the Chinese House Churches to inspire people in the Back to Jerusalem vision. I had the privilege of translating it into English for international distribution, which is carried out by Love China International. When China's Religious Affairs Bureau came into possession of the film, they were so puzzled by its contents that they summoned the director for a meeting to discuss it. What affected them most was the content of the prayers that the team were praying in the film. They couldn't understand why they were praying with such passion and love for the Chinese government when they were supposed to be enemies! *We thought you Christians just wanted to go on pilgrimage to Jerusalem because that's what you do*, they said.

The "Xi'an to Zion" initiative was a crucial moment in the history of the Chinese Church. In the 1940s, the Northwest Spiritual Movement and the Back to Jerusalem Evangelistic Band had attempted this same journey, but their efforts had been frustrated by the newly inaugurated Communist government. Sixty years later, this team of leaders representing millions of Chinese Christians undertook this prophetic–intercessory trip as a way to both spiritually pave the way for the Chinese mission movement and also inspire the Chinese Church with the knowledge that, with God, all things are possible.

Beyond the Middle East

When we talk about the Back to Jerusalem vision, what we are really talking about is one expression of Jesus' Great Commission to the Church, to make disciples of all nations. One of the challenges to the Chinese Church lies in the maturing of their sense of calling. It goes beyond just the Middle East to touch the whole world. The Church has to step up to take responsibility wherever China is gaining influence globally, and one of the most crucial places is the continent of Africa. Over the last decade, China has become the number one investor in Africa. To begin with, there was a strong feeling of optimism about their arrival, just as there is now in the Middle East. Sadly, greed and profiteering has seriously harmed the reputation of Chinese businesses in Africa. They are known for coming into an area, draining the natural resources, and giving very little back to local communities in return. For the Chinese to make an impact through godly business and enterprise in the Middle East, the Church needs to take note of what has happened in Africa and find out what God is calling them to do about it. The calling is on Christian businesspeople to come with a kingdom vision and bring redemption to the mess that has been made by secular Chinese business in the continent. This was the vision of the missionary David Livingstone, who emphasized the partnership between Christianity, civilization, and commerce in seeing the kingdom of God come into every area of society.

One place where we know that this is just now beginning is in Southern Sudan. In 2012 the first Christian missionaries from China came in to lay down their lives and serve the Sudanese people. Elsewhere in China there are those who are sensing God's call to Africa as well as to the Middle East, but this awareness of the bigger picture is still very much in its infancy in the Chinese Church. It is going to be through wider interaction and partnerships with the International Church that China's destiny among the nations is to be more fully realized. For that to take place, there not only need to be open gateways for the gospel to go in and out, but there also needs to be a spiritual authority to decide what comes through those gates. This is the question that the Chinese Church now faces at home: who has the right to be in charge of the spiritual gates?

9

Securing the Gates

We need a breakthrough in government policy if
we are to ever realize the tremendous potential
for future development. We need the space to be
able to grow, just as in other countries.

Dr Ezra Jin, Pastor, Beijing Zion Church

In 2005–2006 there was a great deal of spiritual turbulence
in the Xiaoshan district of the city of Hangzhou, just
south of Shanghai. A House Church network representing
approximately 300,000 believers was having frequent
clashes with the authorities concerning their legal identity
as an unregistered group of churches and the right to
build their own premises. A number of highly successful
entrepreneurs belonging to the church added to their
already substantial influence and purchasing power in the
area. In the end, they set to work constructing a building
as a base to host their weekly meetings and ministry
activities, but the local authorities objected and sent in
a wrecking crew who bulldozed the new building to the

ground. The whole event was secretly filmed by a local, who despite not being a Christian was sympathetic to the church's cause. When they asked him if they could have the video footage as evidence, he agreed and they used it to launch an appeal to the central government. The incident ended up being reported in international news, and the government decided to uphold the appeal case submitted to them by the church. According to a church leader interviewed by Pastor Lee for this book, the network in Xiaoshan was in the end granted permission to construct their own building, and they now have a huge, modern complex serving as one of the first purpose-built House Church buildings in the country.

At Christmas 2007 in the same area, a group of several thousand young people from the church wanted to host an open-air celebration. As they were holding the Christmas procession, a large contingent of Public Security Bureau (PSB) agents came and surrounded them. What happened next is truly remarkable. According to eyewitness accounts, word started to spread quickly throughout the area, which is inhabited by a high percentage of House Church believers. One by one they started coming out of their homes and flanked the police. Before long, as many as 100,000 had gathered, surrounding the police and the few thousand who had gathered for the Christmas celebration. What is even more striking is that there was no violence or angry demonstrations. The believers simply stood their ground praying for the police and the nation. As a result of this encounter, the government sent representatives to talk to the leaders of the network agreeing that they would grant them permission to carry out whatever evangelistic activities they wished. Society had seen something of the momentum carried by God's Church in China, and the paradigm in that local area had shifted. Now they say that in Xiaoshan, if anyone from the church is being harassed by the PSB, one phone call will cause between 30,000 and 50,000 people to come out in support!

... Put walls around them, with towers, gates and bars

Having examined the different stages the Chinese Church has gone through over the last sixty-five years, we are brought to the question of the *bars*. According to the book of Ephesians, the mature Church is one that understands its position of kingdom authority and responsibility. While the gates are necessary for Church to have an outward reformation focus, unsecured gates are dangerous, because while they allow what is of God to flow out into the world, what is of the world can also easily enter in. Perhaps the most crucial stage we are currently witnessing unfold in this grand process is the Church contending for a legal identity within the nation. The Communist Party has reached a point where they acknowledge that the House Churches are far too big and influential to go away, but there is still a battle on an institutional level for the Church's identity. For the first time in history, the Chinese government officially sent representatives to hold a dialogue with House

Church leaders in autumn 2010 concerning what steps could be taken to bring the unregistered churches into a place of legal recognition and protection. Of course, the government still has its own views as to what this would look like, but the very fact that they are willing to talk shows the extent to which things have changed. To quote Ezra Jin, *The development of the urban house churches that started after 1990 has now pierced through the blockades and barriers that the government has set up and has become rooted in almost every area of China's society.*

Several factors have meant that the new Urban House Churches are now becoming positioned more than ever to exert influence in the nation.

First of all, the majority of the leaders of these churches are highly educated, with master's or doctoral level degrees no longer uncommon. Many of them have studied or have connections abroad, and they are also able to articulate a well-developed theology and statement of faith both to their members and to the rest of the world. These leaders find it much easier to engage with the legal and political spheres than their counterparts from the older generation.

Secondly, the whole ethos of these churches is different from what we have classically understood from the Rural House Church. Three-quarters of their members are high school graduates, and nearly two-thirds are under thirty-five years old. They have adopted an active and engaging stance towards social reformation rather than a passive one, and they have been inspired by successful models of church internationally to structure their ministry in a much more holistic way, placing just as much emphasis on pastoral care as on simple evangelistic activity.

Thirdly, they are not afraid to present a united front in actively campaigning for a change in the law and continuing to keep the discussion of religious freedoms in the open. China is still changing fast, and according to Professor Li Fan from the World and China Institute, it has been the influence of Christian intellectuals that has brought the concept of freedom of religion and freedom of thought to the forefront of China's civil rights movement. He also points out that the House Church accounts for one million of the approximately five million NGOs currently active in China, establishing the Christian community as the largest single independent group representing charities and developmental organizations in the country. The Church already carries great influence in the charity and voluntary sector, but for change to be genuinely sustainable there needs to be a voice in the political sphere.

Protests and Politics

From late February to March 2011, the Arab Spring sparked a wave of pro-democracy protests in China. Dubbed the Jasmine Revolution, the protest movement took place on a relatively small scale, but managed to spread to several major cities in China through the use of social media. Frightened of the potential for anti-government sentiment to be stirred up around the country, police and security personnel were called in to try to bring any demonstrations to a quick end. Nevertheless, a viral campaign of dissidence spread throughout the whole Internet, seriously worrying the Chinese regime. With a population accounting for almost a fifth of the entire world, there is no such thing in China as a "small change". Perhaps this is one reason why the government has been suspicious of the Church in the past. Historically, China has more than once seen radical upheaval with some of the world's largest and bloodiest revolts. By way of example, as many as thirty-six million people may have lost their lives as a result of General An Lushan's rebellion against the Tang emperor in AD 755, while at least twenty million died in the Taiping Rebellion between 1850 and 1864 when Hong Xiuquan, claiming to be the younger brother of Jesus, attempted to establish a violent theocratic state in south-eastern China. With such a history of mass uprisings, the thing that the Chinese government fears most of all is social instability.

Set on edge by the Jasmine Revolution movement, the central government launched a crackdown against illegal church activity. One church in particular was singled out as a kind of figurehead representing the whole House Church movement. This was the Church of the Watchmen, or *Shouwang Jiaohui*, in Beijing, led by Pastor Jin Tianming. Shouwang was one of the first fellowships to purchase its own property to use as a church meeting place. Having begun as a small home meeting of a dozen or so members, the fellowship had in a few short years increased to several thousand strong. By the beginning of 2010, the Communist Party had decided that this Urban

House Church was becoming a symbol to the national church networks of the new boldness and authority in the body of Christ when dealing with the government. PSB agents threatened the landlord of an office block they were renting for their church meetings and forced him to evict the congregation. In response, several hundred members met day after day in the open air for an entire month in sub-zero temperatures. The Party caved in and said they would be allowed to purchase their own building if they would stop the open-air meetings. Within a few months the church had paid in full for a large, modern complex in Beijing; but when they tried to move in, government agents blocked their entry and refused to release the keys to them, so they returned to the streets, meeting out in the open. This time the response was fiercer. Shortly after the Jasmine Revolution, key leaders were put under house arrest and young professionals who were members of the church were forced out of their jobs. A few individuals were even detained in prison for several nights. In the midst of this, a coalition of House Church leaders submitted an open petition to the government challenging the mistreatment of these believers and urging a full review of the legal policy on unregistered churches.

This situation remains unresolved at the time of writing. Pastor Lee was able to see Jin Tianming while he was under house arrest, but they were quickly joined by PSB agents who had been monitoring them and they had to call the meeting short. The policy of the Chinese government is still that unregistered churches should join the Three-Self movement in order to be legally recognized, while the position of the Urban House Church leaders challenging this policy is that forcing them to be governed by a secular, atheistic institution is a violation of their religious freedom guaranteed by Article 36 of the Chinese Constitution. They also argue that the TSPM itself is an outdated system from fifty years ago and needs to be reconsidered for a modern and open China. Despite the differences between the House and Three-Self churches, however, huge changes have come in the wake of waves of spiritual renewal passing through the TSPM. In meeting with the pastor of Suzhou Lion Church, a TSPM church near Shanghai, Pastor Lee asked them directly if they adhere to TSPM policy or to the Bible, to which he replied, *To the Bible of course!* In another unusual situation, the leader of a TSPM church recently contacted an Urban House Church pastor in Shenzhen 250 km away and asked them to be the apostolic covering for their ministry. The pastor now periodically travels to preach in the TSPM church, each time fasting and praying for a two-week period in preparation.

There have been rumours circulating among the House Churches that the wife of recently inaugurated Chinese President Xi Jinping is in fact a Christian believer. While it is at present impossible to verify this rumour, what makes it noteworthy is that for anyone even to consider the possibility of such a high-profile political figure being a Christian in China shows just how much things are changing. Similarly, the former Chinese Premier Wen Jiabao has for a long time been said to have had historic ties with the Christian faith.

An article written by the Chinese magazine *Gospel Herald* in March 2013 cited an interview with a pastor close to the former premier who claimed that not only were Wen Jiabao and his family practising Christians themselves, but that Wen's grandfather was actually an early pioneer missionary! The highest-profile convert to Christianity we can be definitely sure of was in fact Premier Wen's personal assistant, who resigned his position after publicly declaring his faith in the national press. More and more testimonies are coming from church leaders who have relationships with Zhongnanhai (the Communist Party's HQ in Beijing) that a number of senior politicians are secretly Christians or at least have a high respect for Christianity and the position of the Church within society. However, there is still a big conflict between those in government in favour of legalizing China's House Churches and those opposed.

God's Kingdom in the Media

Adding to the strange paradoxes which arise when you examine the state of faith in China, Christianity is increasingly in the national media in a positive light. China Central Television (CCTV) is the main network of television and news channels in the country. With all senior staff appointed by the government, it has been accused of being a mouthpiece of government propaganda in the nation. According to a director who was a former employee of CCTV, as of 2002 there were only 15 known Christians out of an organization of 10,000. By 2010 this number had risen to 350. In the 2013 Spring Festival celebration special broadcast on CCTV, one performer even sang a Christian hymn written by an artist called Xiaomin. This is not the only time that Xiaomin's songs have featured in the public eye either. A 2012 film by Chinese director Feng Xiaogang called *Back to 1942* not only openly explores themes of Christian faith in China under the Japanese occupation, but the director specifically chose one of Xiaomin's hymns called *The River of Life* as the theme song to accompany the end credits. Feng is not a Christian believer, but he described his experience of visiting churches in the West on the Chinese social networking site Weibo:

> *Whenever I go abroad and see the churches I am always filled with the desire to go inside and sit for a while. There is something about their grandeur and the sense of peace. I'm not a believer myself, but as soon as I go in and sit down inside one of them, it awakens an awe and reverence inside me. I'm reminded of how profoundly I have sinned in my life...*

In June 2012, a fifteen-minute featurette entitled *Noah's Ark is Not a Myth* was broadcast on the state-controlled television channel, Beijing Television (BTV). The documentary followed a recent expedition that had claimed to discover the remains of Noah's Ark on Mount Ararat in Turkey, and included a short computer-animated film about the story of Noah's flood. During the documentary, it was stated that, *In the ancient world God provided a means of salvation which was the ark. Today in the twenty-first century, God has provided another means of salvation which is in Jesus Christ. Christ is the Noah's Ark of today.* The news anchor ended the programme with the simple statement, *There you have it – Noah's Ark isn't a fairytale after all!*

Many in the Urban House Churches are responding to these positive signs in the press and popular culture by actively encouraging people to engage with social media to communicate the gospel and voice their opinion on social issues. There is an understanding among the new generation of leadership that instead of adopting a siege mentality towards society, the Church can take pride of place in shaping its direction. While China is not a democracy as we understand it in the West, there are gradually more platforms emerging for Chinese people to air their views openly through the Internet. Even the government is turning to social networking sites such as Weibo to communicate its message and to take the pulse of national opinion.

One poll organized in March 2013 by the government asked the question, *Do you believe that China should legalize same-sex marriage?* Out of the 10,000 people who responded to the poll, only one-third was against the legalization of same-sex marriage – which is in itself an insight into the changing attitudes towards social morals in Chinese society – but what makes the poll significant as far as this book is concerned is that in reading through the comments made by those in favour, a disproportionately high number specifically attacked Christianity and the Christian view of marriage in making their arguments. This shows that Christian ethics have already become influential enough among the emerging generation to be considered a relevant part of the discussion.

As well as diffusing throughout the secular arena, the Church is also finding its own voice through specifically Christian media. In 2010, two online publications produced from the same head office in Beijing – the *Gospel Times* and the *Christian Times* – began to be promoted nationally and internationally. These are entirely funded and supported by Christians inside China, with over twenty full-time staff and a web design company to generate income for the ministry. The company has managed to become officially recognized by the government as both a legal entity and a Christian media company. Their stated aims are threefold: to provide a record of God's work in China; to be a window for the Chinese Church to society; and to be a platform for preaching the gospel. For the first time in history, China's House Churches have a voice through which they can communicate internationally. The majority of the readership is still from Mainland China, but increasingly readers from all over the world are visiting the websites. They are very willing to talk openly about the Christian faith, while also giving a Christian perspective on social issues such as films, current affairs, and politics.

Marketplace Missionaries

There is a saying in China that if you have enough money you can even get a ghost to grind the mill; in other words, money talks. The Chinese have historically been a culture of merchants, preferring to establish their influence through trade rather than military strength. For many Chinese Church leaders, the lack of legal recognition within society has meant that they have turned to business as a way to bring in financial provision for them and their churches. Building successful businesses with a kingdom ethos is crucial to seeing the Church's influence and position in society grow. Modern Chinese culture has become one of the most consumerist and capitalist in the world today, and there is now more need than ever for a Christian testimony in the business world.

While the gospel is making inroads into the political, educational, and cultural spheres, it is also taking the business world by storm. The head of the Zhejiang Chamber of Commerce was suffering from diabetes and terminal cancer. He went to see Pastor Rong from Shanghai on the recommendation of a friend. Rong went to his house several times to pray for him, and he came to stay for a fortnight at the healing centre in Shanghai. Each time he was prayed for he noticed substantial improvement until in the end he was completely healed. He is a well-known and well-respected business leader in his region, as well as being a member of the Communist Party. As a result of his healing, he decided to become a Christian and now he is very open about his newly found Christian faith, frequently sharing how God healed him in answer to prayer with his associates in the Chamber of Commerce! When Pastor Lee met him he had a taste for the passion for the gospel that this man spread everywhere. He didn't stop giving thanks to God for saving his life, and was very happy for us to use his testimony in the book.

If you go to Shanghai you might stumble across a very unusual coffee shop called Teddy Beloved. The owner is a Christian businessman whose wife studied interior design and has a particular fondness for teddy bears. They felt that God was calling them to use their skills and interests to set up a business that could be a vehicle for kingdom values to become a blessing to society. Having been in business for the last seven years, the Teddy Beloved coffee shop has grown to be one of the most famous cafes in Shanghai. As well as being covered with just about every kind of teddy bear you can imagine, the shop is also filled with crosses, Christian artwork, and Scriptures. When they first started, only one of the staff was a believer; now every one of the two dozen employees has become a Christian. The shop is famous for giving customers the opportunity to custom-design their own teddy bear while they sit and have a coffee. Every bear they produce has a tag on it with the verses from 1 Corinthians 13:4–8 all about love, and company policy is that when staff serve coffee to a customer, they also briefly share their testimony! A businessman from Taiwan who wasn't a Christian heard about the shop and came over to investigate. Having interviewed all the staff and looked over their business model, he couldn't understand how the business was making such a gigantic profit. The owner's response was that he simply listens to the Holy Spirit and does what He says, so the business is a success. As a result of visiting the shop, the businessman from Taiwan concluded that it must be God who was blessing the business, so he also decided to become a Christian.

The coffee shop doubles up as a church with the employees as the congregation. Originally they held Sunday worship services, but they were forced to stop when other shop owners complained to the authorities that the owner was a member of a cult and was spreading superstition around the area. Now they still keep a small group fellowship and Bible study for the staff during the week. Teddy Beloved is the longest surviving business on that street, much to the jealousy of the neighbouring shop owners. The owner has five areas of ministry where the cafe is having a substantial effect. The first group they focus on is the staff. They led all of the staff to Christ and continue to disciple them through the business. Secondly, they want to reach their customers. People from all over China and abroad come to visit the shop because of its reputation. The ethos is that everyone who comes is touched by the love of God. Thirdly, the owner has set up an informal meeting of other business people related to the Full Gospel Business Men's Fellowship in Shanghai where they can have a meal together and hear the gospel in a low-key way. This ministry is aimed at reaching the "elites" in society with the gospel. Fourthly, they have a model of outreach that places a high value on ministering to the poor. They realized that in Europe, a handmade teddy bear can sell for several thousand euros, so by actively recruiting disabled people who otherwise cannot get work, they teach them how to make bears and give them a means to earn a good living. Finally, they have made the offer to Christians in universities and colleges that if they run any evangelistic activities, the shop will supply them with handmade teddy bears free of charge to give to anyone who responds to the gospel as a way of welcoming people into the kingdom. On top of all this, in November 2013, they will be working with the local government to host the very first teddy bear exhibition in Shanghai.

Testimonies like this show just what can be possible when we follow God's leading and vision for our lives. It seems likely that this new breed of missionaries in the business world will be instrumental in building bridges for the gospel both inside China and beyond. God created nature to abhor a vacuum, and I think that this reflects something of His nature. Whatever we yield to Him, He will fill with His grace and presence. The Chinese Church is beginning to recognize that there is no separation between spiritual and secular life, but that Christ wants to fill all of it with His glory and goodness. Our own skills and interests are infinitely valuable to Him if we just allow Him to fill them! The believers of the Chinese Church are genuinely expecting the gospel to overtake the entire nation of China. There is still a long way to go, and there are still many obstacles to be overcome, but China's kingdom momentum seems to be like a runaway train rolling down a hill and out into the nations.

10

Looking to the Future

In 1949, the Chinese Church was forcibly separated from the West by the Communist Party, but in the Spirit we have remained one family. China's Open Door Policy has now allowed a reconnection to take place between the Churches of East and West, so that we can go out together and fulfil the Back to Jerusalem Vision.

Pastor Jin Tianming, Beijing Shouwang Church

The Drought is Ending

And Elijah said to Ahab, "Go, eat and drink, for there is the sound of a heavy rain." So Ahab went off to eat and drink, but Elijah climbed to the top of Carmel, bent down to the ground and put his face between his knees. "Go and look

173

toward the sea," he told his servant. And he went up and looked. "There is nothing there," he said. Seven times Elijah said, "Go back." The seventh time the servant reported, "A cloud as small as a man's hand is rising from the sea." So Elijah said, "Go and tell Ahab, 'Hitch up your chariot and go down before the rain stops you.'"

(1 Kings 18:41–44)

God called Elijah and the widow together to help each other during the season of drought. Like the widow, the Chinese Church has not yet come through to full breakthrough in the nation and is still facing spiritual drought in the form of opposition from the state. Meanwhile, the churches of the West and especially Europe have also been feeling the effects of a drought of a different kind. Many are confronting a so-called "post-Christian society", and have become defensive, as when Elijah became intimidated by the evil Queen Jezebel and ran away to hide in the desert. Yet the drought only exists for a season. Elijah rose up again by the grace of God, and the lives of the widow and her son continued after the coming of the rain. China is close to the end of its long season of drought, but many of the leaders we interviewed still believe that there will be one final wave of persecution, which will cause the Chinese Church to truly step into her destiny. The younger generation knows very little of the hardships experienced by the former generations, but those years of fierce opposition helped to shape the Chinese House Churches into what they are today. It is part of their *chuancheng* – their spiritual inheritance. This is why they believe that the situation with Shouwang Church and others like it has still not been resolved. A final wave of refining is coming as the forces within the government that are opposed to the Church try one last time to fight directly against it. If this does break out into another wave of institutional persecution, it will not last long and it is highly unlikely to involve the kind of violent imprisonments of the past, but it will be enough to remind the new generation that their God is more powerful than any force that can come against them, and He will deliver them.

There is a growing feeling that some of the attempts by the Urban House Churches to emulate a Western/Korean megachurch model are pushing in the wrong direction. When All Nations Church in Shanghai experienced a crackdown similar to Shouwang in Beijing, it caused them to go back to their roots as a House Church movement, meeting together in small groups in each other's homes instead of in a large Sunday congregation. In this current season, it seems that most of the churches that have come under attack from the government are Urban House Churches. God has a real desire for the Chinese Church to retain their strong emphasis on meeting together organically in small groups. This is not to say that the larger-scale church structures are wrong, but that, regardless of the size of the congregation or the ministry, they have to be true to the spiritual DNA of their past. Since the days of Watchman Nee, John Song, and Wang Mingdao, no church leaders have stood out as having the same degree of influence as these patriarchs. God is keeping the focus on every member of the body of Christ in China being activated and released into their full potential, and He seems to be protecting the Church from congregations becoming passive recipients of the pastor's ministry.

When Elijah prayed at the top of Mount Carmel for the rain to come, he first made a bold declaration to King Ahab: *Go eat and drink for there is the sound of a heavy rain.* Elijah heard the sound in the Spirit before there was any physical sign of a change. Right now across the nations of the world there is a sound of a heavy rain of revival, greater than anything that has happened before. We need to be sensitive to what the Holy Spirit is saying and get ready to cooperate with it. Rain is coming on the land in China, but until it comes the Chinese Church must recognize that they are still facing the final stages of drought. Just as God called Elijah and the widow together, the Chinese Church and the Western Church have a message for each other.

Even with a degree of institutional opposition, Christianity in China is still turning the nation upside down. Even with a government and educational system that is ideologically based on atheism, it is not stopping the Church presenting a powerful, transformative witness to society. Many believers in the Western Church are concerned about laws restricting their religious freedoms. They are on the defensive, afraid that they will be overtaken by Islam or secularism alike. The message to the West is a call to consider China's example in remembering how to pray, how to believe, and being mindful of the Church's own identity and calling in each season of time. Our inheritance in the West includes generations of world-changing revival history – our own *chuancheng*. We have to recognize and embrace the legacy of former generations in order to recover our identity in society and position in God's plans. Revival has been sweeping a nation with a far more hostile legal system than any in the West! The Chinese Church meanwhile is in need of the wisdom and impartation of spiritual fathers from the Western Church. They also need the Western Church to pray like Elijah for the end of the drought. It is only through embracing true partnership in the kingdom and in recognizing each other's complementary strengths that we can fully see God's purposes accomplished on earth.

A Message of Unity

In most big cities now, pastors and leaders in the House Churches from across the area have for the last few years developed the practice of gathering together regularly to pray and encourage one another. In Beijing, the Leaders' Forum has been meeting monthly since 2007. The chairman of the Beijing forum is called Pastor Wang, and when we asked him what the biggest challenge facing pastors in China today is, he replied *loneliness*. "Pastor" is not considered a valid career in China, and being a House Church pastor is not even a legal career. In the early days of his ministry, Pastor Wang wouldn't dare to tell others outside of the Church what he did for a living. In his *xiaoqu* community, people would say to him, *How come you're never at work and yet you have a car? What do you do anyway?* He could only reply that he was a *freelancer*.

Church leaders still find that it is very difficult to have close friends, especially as pastors are considered to be holy and set apart and it is therefore difficult for them to share openly with others, even other leaders. "Face-saving" in Chinese culture makes it even more difficult for people to be genuinely honest with one another. Their family life is often affected, and there is a very real and present fear that they might at any time be arrested and taken away, so they try to spend as much time with their children as they can. Church pastors are referred to as *cult leaders* by the Public Security Bureau (PSB) and Religious Affairs Bureau. There's no doubt that every House Church pastor is known to the authorities, and government agents will routinely attend church meetings to keep track of what is going on. Expectations on leaders are very high, and many feel as if they are on call 24–7. Sometimes the demands of the ministry and mission trips to other areas can take them away from home for weeks at a time. This puts a great strain on relationships with their spouses and children. Marriage counselling and "couples camps" have become a new way in China to help strengthen these relationships and teach people how to relate more healthily towards family and friends.

For example, Pastor Lee interviewed two theological students whose families can't understand why they would throw away their expensive education to do something that is not accepted in society, and with no guarantee of income. Finances are a huge pressure particularly on young leaders who are the only children in their families, as they are expected by society to be the main source of income for retired parents and grandparents. Pastor Wang considers himself blessed that as a pastor he receives approximately 3,000 yuan (£300) a month in income, but in Beijing the minimum a person can expect to pay in rent now is 2,000 yuan (£200) a month. Raising children in China's modern cities is very expensive, and pastors' children can often be a subject of bullying from their peers because they don't have the latest phone or brand name shoes or clothes. The practice of taking an offering is not common in Chinese churches, and they are having to learn how to better administer the finances and support those who are dedicating themselves full-time to church ministry.

As well as all of this, the pressure in ministry is getting greater and greater as educational levels are rising. Pastors need to invest more time in furthering their own study to keep up. More and more pastors have master's or doctorate degrees, and this is a very new trend. The challenges presented by modern urban life have created a much more complex environment, and the lifestyles, cultures, and backgrounds of the congregation members are much more diverse than historically in the rural churches. This inevitably brings with it all sorts of divisions, both within churches and between churches.

One River, Many Streams

The three main branches of the Protestant House Church each carry a unique spirituality that is of tremendous value to the others. As well as these, we have yet to see the role the Catholic House Churches and Three-Self churches will play in China's future spiritual landscape. What is clear, however, is that each of these streams belongs to a single river that is greater than the sum of its parts.

The Traditional House Church has a strong emphasis on perseverance under trial, and the development of personal, intimate relationship with God. While there are stories of individuals who abandoned the faith under the strongest period of opposition between 1949 and 1979, the Church as a whole stood firm. The long, hard winter caused them to place a high value on cultivating the inner spiritual life, as is shown clearly in the writings of Watchman Nee. At a time when noise is constantly increasing, developing a true quietness of soul is a rare and profound testimony, and of immense value to the modern Church.

The Rural House Church, meanwhile, is the only group that has widespread experience in trans-regional evangelism and church planting. Although they were equipped with just a handful of sermons and the most basic doctrinal knowledge, the movement was founded on the preaching of a simple message and praying for the sick to be healed. Their heritage is that of mass evangelism, seeing more people come to faith between 1979 and 1999 than at any other period in China's history. What they stand for is a pure and childlike faith in a God who works miracles. That simplicity of faith and missional focus will be a great asset in the continuing work of evangelizing China and the Back to Jerusalem vision.

Finally, the Urban House Church is seeking to raise up a contextualized model of church which can engage meaningfully with twenty-first-century China. They have a strong culture of discipleship and pastoral care, and carry a commitment to social reformation. With many members having a high degree of education, social status, or financial assets, the Urban Church is able to experiment with different shapes and models of church, and of the three it is by far the best placed to deal head-on with the authorities. Their administrative abilities and growing international connections – especially with the South Korean Church – mean that their input is vital in sustaining and maturing the move of God in China.

The coming shift in relationship between Church and state brings a different set of challenges, however, and the ongoing success of China's churches lies in building local congregations that are full of life and able to continue to meet the spiritual needs of the people to whom they are supposed to be ministering. As these three generations of church work out what true unity looks like between them, China will be prepared for the next step.

The Land

After the building of the walls, towers, gates, and bars, 2 Chronicles 14:7 ends with a statement concerning the land: "The land is still ours, because we have sought the LORD our God; we sought him and he has given us rest on every side." So they built and prospered. The potential exists for China to become the world's largest and most influential Christian nation. Before that can happen, a number of major obstacles must be overcome, not least of which is the legal status of the House Church. The Chinese authorities are still continuing to discuss how to give legal recognition to the unregistered churches, and the State Department held another major consultation to look at this question in July 2013. In many ways the outcome is not unexpected. There has been no significant shift in policy, but the government has more formally expressed that it is keeping an eye on the city of Wenzhou in the East of China as a testing ground for granting more freedoms to the House Church. Wenzhou is already known for having a very strong and active Christian presence. Whatever the outcome, they are getting ready to respond. The Church's vision is to become the main force of world mission within the next twenty or thirty years, but it is only when revival is seen again on a scale comparable to the 1980s and 1990s that the House Church will be able to take part sustainably in world mission. This is what they are contending for.

Shen Xianfeng's prophetic insight combined with an analysis of the last sixty-five years of China's history foresees three seasons for the future. The first season is what we are currently seeing taking place today – the evangelization of the nations' cities. The Urban House Church is very influential but still relatively small in numbers. With possibly 10 per cent of the population adhering to the Christian faith in one form or another, the task of reaching people within China's borders is still huge. He predicts that this will remain the primary focus until about 2019. During this period many leaders expect mass evangelization to be catalysed by a final wave of institutional persecution, with the end result that the House Churches become fully established in their spiritual and legal identity. The evolution of China's charitable and NGO sector will provide more opportunity for the Church to *register in the hearts of the people* in expressing the love of God in practical ways, and work to heal society through bringing reformation into all the major spheres of cultural influence. Once this has taken place, the spotlight will turn to China's western regions, especially to Xinjiang and Tibet. The decade beginning in 2020 will see a vehicle for cross-cultural mission becoming visible, with fully trained missionaries operating under the banners of commerce and development work among China's minorities. By 2029, the Church is expected to be finally ready to present a powerful and credible solution to the Middle East in going out to fulfil the Back to Jerusalem vision in partnership with the International Church. For Shen, *the future of the Chinese Church lies in doing it right, doing it bigger, and doing it better.*

China's Message

Our vision needs to expand. The Western Church has many times been guilty of having a very European/American centric view of what God is doing in the world. The Chinese Church needs to be careful that it does not make the same mistake of allowing a seed of nationalism to be mixed in with their understanding of the gospel. The whole political and spiritual landscape of the globe is about to change over the next fifty years even more radically than it has done over the twentieth century. There will always be people who fear change and prophets who claim that the end of the world is at hand simply because their small and brief world is giving way to a new one. The Chinese Church has maintained the firm conviction that God is in charge and He knows what He is doing. They have grown in an environment with nothing to lose and everything to gain. In the West, Christians tend to panic whenever something threatens our "freedoms". Especially in the charismatic/Pentecostal churches, there is far too much debate about which political leader of the hour might be the antichrist or whether or not the European Union is the embodiment of all things evil. We must stop cursing Europe and start blessing it! God's agenda is to revive the Old World in a greater way than ever before because *the gifts and calling of God are irrevocable*.

In 1947 the great revivalist Smith Wigglesworth prophesied a wave of revival sweeping across the whole of Europe and culminating in the greatest move of God ever to have been seen. He prophesied what he could see, but having had the benefit of over sixty-five years of world history we have been given the opportunity to view an even bigger picture. There is a new move of God that is in its infancy in Europe, but it will rise to become something that is not owned by one particular nation or stream of Church. There is a call to equal partnership across the global Church from *every tribe and language*. We are about to see a shift where the apostolic and prophetic voice of the Chinese Church is going to be heard across the whole world. It will no longer be the case that ministries and missions pour in a single direction towards a suffering Chinese Church which needs our help, but there will equally be an outflow of mutual support and impartation spilling over China's borders.

There are several things which the Chinese Church has modelled to us and which are like the widow's sustenance given to Elijah in the time of drought.

First of all, they understand the need for a genuine spirit of unity. In many places Satan has not only divided the Church through hundreds of doctrinal and denominational disputes, but he has also shattered it by bringing division between the generations. There must be a horizontal unity between church streams and a vertical unity between generations which is able to honour and value what each part supplies while also recognizing the distinctiveness and uniqueness of the others. Without this our *chuancheng* gets short-circuited – we forget what God has done in the past and so we lose perspective on our future. It also causes us to be vulnerable to an orphan spirit, where our view of God the Father becomes distorted by a works-based mentality that has more to do with religion and servitude than sonship. The heart of the Father is love and wants to soak us with that love so that whoever comes anywhere near us gets wet!

Second, the Chinese Church has not allowed political or social obstacles to be an issue. Has Europe experienced a spiritual decline? Is the American Church facing more institutional opposition than perhaps ever before? Whatever roadblocks have come in our path, the Chinese Church has had even more. The biggest enemy facing the Western and Eastern churches alike is neither Islam nor secularism but lukewarm Christianity. While bringing kingdom influence into government is important, let us not forget that the greatest period of spiritual growth in China came in the 1980s and 1990s when the Church had no political voice at all. The problems come when, like Elijah with Jezebel, we pay more attention to what is going on around us than to what God is doing. That becomes a source of intimidation for us, paralysing our ability to release life and love to a hurting world. If we really know who our God is, then there is no need to fear the opposing voices of judges or politicians. It's just as my friend in Beijing said, *If you fear God, you don't have to fear the government!*

Third, there is a call both on China and from China for believers to pursue intimacy with God as the utmost priority. Watchman Nee said that the worst place for a Christian to be is in a state where he or she is not hungry for God. We have inherited a kingdom that is *righteousness, peace, and joy in the Holy Spirit*, but the way many believers talk you would think that this was a kingdom of guilt, striving, and morbid depression! The Chinese Church has been able to thrive because there are deep roots and foundations underneath. In his endorsement of this book, Brother Yun spoke of the Chinese Church being like a spiritual Isaac to our Abraham, helping to dig out the deep wells, which have been allowed to become blocked. We have an incredible spiritual history that can be opened back up to us both corporately and as individuals. Let's not settle for the shallows when God is inviting us into the open sea.

Finally, we can allow ourselves to be reminded that faith is actually a very simple thing. We do the simple, and God does the complex. The Chinese Church is built on simple, pragmatic faith. Especially in the Rural House Church revivals, their ministry consisted of simply listening to the Holy Spirit and doing what He told them to do. That same DNA has been transmitted through into China's House Churches of today. Rather than look at all the reasons why something can't work, we have talked about some of the stories in which ordinary men and women are taking the little that is in their hands and acting on it in faith. Hope is one of the eternally enduring virtues of the kingdom of God. What the world needs more than ever is hope, but unless we are living from a place of joyful hope and confident expectancy, we will have nothing to offer the world than religious platitudes and rehearsed sayings. The message of the Chinese Church is a message of hope: God is able to do ridiculously, staggeringly more than anything we could ever conjure up in our minds to ask Him to do, and He is willing to do it because He has already put His power in us to do it! May this book open up a new perspective not just on China but on your own calling and destiny in Christ.

Love China International

Love China International began in 2003 as the BTJ Foundation UK, which later merged with Life Impact Ministries in 2009. The ministry was founded to support the Chinese House Church in their Back to Jerusalem vision following a series of meetings across the UK with Brother Yun. We have been sharing the vision with Churches and organizations across the UK and Europe, funding the development of a training programme for Chinese Christian workers while providing support to Chinese Christians already working cross-culturally both inside and outside China. We are linking the Chinese House Church with Christian organizations worldwide to help develop friendships and partnerships between East and West in the task of fulfilling the Great Commission.

In addition to our ministry within China, we work among the Chinese communities in the UK and Europe, organizing worship and praise gatherings, short-term-missions, and an annual conference for Chinese and European believers. Some of the projects supported by LCI in China and Europe are as follows:

A Special School to provide a proper education for disadvantaged and disabled children in China which has helped numerous children secure work in local businesses and farms, etc;

A centre for training Chinese pastors and cross-cultural workers;

A Prayer Healing Centre to minister to terminally ill patients on whom doctors have given up hope. The centre cares for them by providing free food and lodging and prayer ministry. Hundreds have been healed and brought into the Kingdom of God, including high ranking officials;

European Short-Term Mission, partnering with local Chinese churches evangelizing restaurant workers and students from the overseas Chinese communities;

An annual European Life Impact Conference bringing Chinese Christians together and helping them to develop a real and personal relationship with the loving heavenly Father, and to fulfill their calling as Christian disciples.

Contact Love China International

55 James Street
Oxford
OX4 1EU
United Kingdom

Telephone: +44 (1865) 432-703
Email: office@lcinternational.org
Website: http://www.lcinternational.org